In P. ..... .j . ...s

In his memoir *First Years*, Ed Demerly opens a window on the past, showing in vivid detail what life was like in the '40s, '50s and '60s. Viewing his life on a farm, in a small Michigan town, in a family of seven, we see the constant work, the family dynamics, and communitarian practices. In the garret bedroom he shared with his brothers, "We boys used to practice writing out alphabet letters with our fingernails in the frost on the roof boards." Demerly remembers "the chickens singing and sunning themselves and cackling their deliveries in the winter coop." The values and discipline he learns on the farm support him at each stage of life—at the university, in the military and Army Ranger training, in the Peace Corps, and through his adult and professional life. This compelling American story will be of interest to anyone who contemplates writing their life.

~ Rick Bailey, author of *Get Thee to a Bakery*, a memoir in essays

Ed Demerly's *First Years* is one of the most artistically sketched and moving memoirs of our time. All narrative situations carry reflective weight, description, and passion. His story begins with the true dynamics of his past life as a shy, obedient American farm boy who later joins the army, Peace Corps, and higher ed where he worked for over forty years. It ends with understanding and acceptance.

~ Mary Saad Assel, PhD, Henry Ford College, retired educator and author

Ed Demerly's youth on an impoverished farm reflects a culture, which no longer exists in America. While many memoirs may have interesting anecdotes, Ed's are so much more inviting as they are written with such great feeling. His book truly brought this reader to tears, especially as he writes of his relationships with his family members. Ed's subtle, self-deprecating humor keeps the reader engaged. Even his punctuation brings deep meaning to his stories. My one complaint: I wanted the story of Ed's life to go on and on. The book truly is a page turner.

~ L. Glenn O'Kray, historian, editor,
 retired college instructor and administrator

Like *Hillbilly Elegy, First Years* offers readers insights into a way of life in America that will be foreign to most readers. While *Hillbilly Elegy* tells a story of Appalachia and the author's successful escape from the whirlpool of poverty, abuse, and dysfunction, *First Years* shows readers what it was like to grow up in a large farm family where hard work and Christian values shape every day, where all individuals contribute to the family's survival, and where parents and community are the lynchpins of life. *First Years* takes readers on a journey of the author's formative early years — including a life-changing bout of rheumatic fever — through his world-broadening experiences as the first in his family to attend college and his later work in the US Army and in the Peace Corps. Deeply personal but with familiar touchstones of the middle twentieth century — the Kennedy presidency and the peace movement — the memoir offers readers a true experience of the writer's lifelong growth through personal challenges, tragedies, and successes.

~ Linda Di Desidero, PhD,
University of Maryland Global Campus

In this well executed volume, Ed Demerly describes his initial farm years and his later years as an army ranger and Peace Corps volunteer with arresting detail. This farm boy can write. The chapter, "Sinking Deep in Sin," provides the interpretive key to the book. Ed had drifted from the faith of his early years. Decades later, he asked for renewed faith so that his second marriage might be made right. He had scarcely asked for this blessing when he found that he had received it!

~ Fr. Richard J. Cassidy, Professor of
Sacred Scripture, Sacred Heart Major Seminary

FIRST YEARS

A Farm Boy
Faces the Future

My kindergarten picture.

Ed Demerly

FIRST YEARS
A Farm Boy
Faces the Future

A MEMOIR

Mission Point Press

First Years: A Memoir

A Farm Boy Faces the Future

Copyright @2021 by Ed Demerly

All world rights reserved.

Readers are encouraged to go to www.MissionPointPress. com to contact the author or to find information on how to buy this book in bulk at a discounted rate.

Published by Mission Point Press
2554 Chandler Rd.
Traverse City, MI 49696
(231) 421-9513
MissionPointPress.com

ISBN: 9781954786363

Library of Congress Control Number: 2021912190

Printed in the United States of America

Cover photo: Ed and his older brother Dave, ready for school on Ed's first day of kindergarten.

For my granddaughters —
Brittany, Kara, Brenna, and Caitlin

And for all my nieces and nephews and
grandnieces and grandnephews who represent
a next generation with goals and aspirations to
make the world a better place and in doing so will
be writing their own memoirs.

And in memory of ...

My parents, Dorothy (1919-2001)
and Shirley (1917-1972)

My sister, Judy Stotenbur (1945-2018)

My son, David (1968-2002)

"Love cultivates hope; hope fertilizes resilience, and we can all be farmers of dreams."
— George E. Miller

"The ultimate goal of farming is not the growing of crops, but the cultivation and perfection of human beings." — Masanobu Fukuoka

"The farm is part of me." — Erich Wehrenberg

"O farmers excessively fortunate if only they recognize their blessings." — Virgil

"How ya gonna keep 'em down on the farm (after they've seen Paree)?" — Sam M. Lewis and Joe Young — American songwriters

"The past is never dead. It's not even past." — William Faulkner

"I like a man who likes to see a fine barn as well as a good tragedy." — Ralph Waldo Emerson

"But though an old man, I am but a young gardener." — Thomas Jefferson

"Thank God, I'm a country boy!" — John Denver

Contents

Acknowledgements

I want to thank my teaching colleagues Mary Assel, Nancy Owen Nelson, Rick Bailey, and Glenn O'Kray — all published authors who encouraged me to collect my various memoir essays into one publication. Thanks, too, to John Reddy, who insisted that I continue to set memories onto paper. I also want to thank Peter Putnam for his creative format which I borrowed to describe my parents. Thanks to my grand-niece, Rachel Demerly, for her technical help in editing my manuscript. To Anne Stanton, my editor at Mission Point Press, much gratitude for putting the pieces together so admirably.

Thanks especially to my wife, Martha, who has inspired me to do much more than I ever imagined I could do since the day I met her. Her confident leadership, meticulous preparation, and creative insights have been models I have tried to emulate in both life and writing.

Preface

As is probably true for many memoir writers, these collected essays began as a desire to leave behind bits and pieces of my experience for perhaps a great, great grandson who might discover them sixty years from now and proclaim, "Wow! This guy had a pretty interesting life."

That has been my reaction when on occasion I have found in my mother's collected miscellany, a post card or a faded letter in meticulous handwriting or a photo filled with notes on the back side. They're all remarkable glimpses into ordinary lives that preceded ours. For me, those discoveries have been very few, almost absent from my father's family. Thus, I set out to fill a small portion of that gap.

To a great extent, my early life on a Shiawassee County, Michigan, dairy farm influenced my personality and decisions that directed my life. Except for a year of living on campus only twenty miles from home as a college freshman, I remained at home on the farm until I left for the army at the age of twenty-one. My very limited travel outside Michigan was with my parents and four siblings on camping trips. These essays reveal the experience of a farm boy quite unprepared but eager to face a greater world.

The first essay, *The Demerly Diaspora*, previously published in *Building America; Immigrant Stories of Hope and Hardship*, serves as a brief family history

Andrew and his wife, Magdalena, had seven children. Strangely enough, several of these children were registered on official records with the last name spelled Demerle and the others as Demerly. There were four sons, two named Nicholas. As I understand it, the older Nicholas, my great grandfather, left New York for Benzonia, Michigan, in his early twenties after a family dispute about farm property inheritance. There apparently wasn't enough land to divide among four sons. For generations within the family, there was no discussion about the New York relatives, and none of the family ever returned to visit those relatives. My great grandfather homesteaded land that had been timbered and developed a quite prosperous farm. He donated a small section of his farm for a local one-room school house and in gratitude, the county named the road on which he lived Demerly Road, which still today crosses M-31 about a mile south of Benzonia. His oldest son, Andrew, inherited the farm Nicholas homesteaded.

My father, Shirley, the youngest of Andrew and Josephine's seven children, was twenty-one years younger than his oldest brother. I understand there were a number of miscarriages between live births. After eighth grade, my dad ended his formal education and left that same one-room school his grandfather had donated to the township. I'm told it was because he needed to find work during the Depression, but it may have been that he was tired of his mother's watching his every move in the classroom from her kitchen window. He worked at a dairy, harvested ice from Crystal Lake in winter, cut timber, picked fruit, and worked for other farmers. Eventually, he found work as a farmhand about 100 miles to the south near Owosso, where he met my mother at a barn dance where he was playing guitar in a country band. My mother, Dorothy, was a town girl with a high school education. Her father was a poor country lawyer and county prosecutor who was sometimes paid with chickens and vegetables during the Depression. Her mother was a one-room school teacher before she married. I don't remember either of them because they died when I was very young. They were of Wilson/Ford Scottish ancestors who immigrated before the American revolution; not, however, the Woodrow and Henry branches of the Scottish tree.

My parents returned to Benzonia for a year after their marriage and lived with my grandparents where my older brother was born. With luck in his work as an attorney, Grandpa Wilson was able to find and put a down payment on a foreclosed 120-acre farm near Owosso — a gift for them in place of the college education my mother's three siblings were given. I was the first of their five children born in Owosso in 1941 making me a fourth-generation immigrant. That farm is now managed by my brother, his son, and his grandson.

My father was a phenomenally successful, proud, creative farmer. He was fortunate to be farming in a prosperous post-war 1950s America, but I remember poverty in my first ten years living in a two-room converted granary with a woodburning kitchen stove, one running faucet, an outdoor toilet, an icebox, and a sometimes-leaky roof. My parents started farming with horses and a few chickens, pigs, and dairy cattle. Little by little with increased bank loans which worried my mother, they were able to build a new home and sheds from lumber timbered from the farm and to buy improved machinery and more livestock. With three teenage sons to help with farm work in these years, life improved for all of us. My sisters and mother contributed immeasurably as well, often doing the barn chores during harvest while we were in the fields, not to mention the amounts of laundry, sewing, cooking, trips to town for machinery parts, and bookkeeping. Farm life was a family lifestyle, not a job.

All five of us children — Dave, me, Dick, Jude (Judy), and Sal (Sally) — completed high school. My older brother, David, served in the army then worked for years as a foreman in construction. I completed my master's degree in English after having served in the Army and the Peace Corps. I taught for forty-six years, mostly at Henry Ford College in Dearborn, Michigan. My younger brother, Dick, took over the farm and with the help of his youngest son and now his grandson has expanded the business considerably. My sister Judy worked as a secretary for a congressman and later owned her own seamstress business, then worked in a dental office. My youngest sister, Sally, also owns her own seamstress business making wedding gowns, curtains, and suits and does some missionary work in Brazil and the Philippines.

Among my parents' grandchildren and great grandchildren, fifth and sixth generation immigrants, there are engineers, financial planners, business owners, a horticulturist, a farmer, teachers, an event planner, bankers, a homecare nurse, an office manager, a psychologist, a legal secretary, a policeman, a geologist, a graphic designer, and a construction planner.

In 2006, I visited the small village of Etting, Lorraine, France, the first ancestor of emigres to the USA to return to the village from which they had come

174 years earlier. In 2005, Gilles Demmerle, a distant relative and family genealogist I'd never heard of, contacted me by email inquiring about my ancestry of which I knew almost nothing beyond my parents. He however, knew much — going back about 400 years. When he heard that we planned to travel to Europe the following year, his research of my branch of the Demmerles began in earnest.

He and I first met in the High Tyrol Mountains of Austria and traveled to the mountain village of Strengen where we had dinner with the Tamerl family who had lived at the same home site for over 400 years. When some of that family of stonecutters moved around 1679 to Germany and France after the Thirty Years War during the period of King Louis XIV, their name became Demmerle. Christian Tamerl from Zams, Austria, settled first in Achen, Germany, in1681 then moved to Etting, France, in 1708. Our journey ended at a reunion, to my surprise, in the town hall of Etting with about 200 Demerly relatives, the town mayor, and French public television. I have returned to that village several times since then and have maintained friendships with a number of my new relatives who have also visited the US. On my last visit, while walking in the local cemetery with my wife, Martha, where a third of the plots seemed to be Demmerles, we met another Martha Demmerle visiting a relative's grave. It's a small world.

My family's immigration story isn't complete without including my adopted Korean daughter, Angela, who arrived at age four in 1975, just as American involvement in the Vietnam War was ending. Even before her arrival, I sensed some of the racial resent-

2

Born to Life on a Farm

By fate, I was born to a farmer and his farm wife in late fall 1941 just three weeks before the bombing of Pearl Harbor. Two years before, my two-year-old brother, Dave moved with my parents from Benzonia to the farm on the corner of Brewer and Ruess Roads halfway between Owosso and Perry in Shiawassee County. Grandpa Wilson, a Depression-era lawyer in Owosso, had, with a mortgage down payment, procured the 120-acre farm for them at a foreclosure sale. I guess it was Ma's college money since her brothers and sister all went to college, but she chose adventure and marriage to my farmer dad soon after high school.

The farm was fertile and relatively flat with a generous drainage ditch running through it. It had a fairly large woods at the back of a lowland muck pasture. There was an old orchard, a standard Michigan barn in need of repair, a chicken coop, and an outhouse. Because I was born at Owosso Memorial Hospital, I can't say that I was born in a log cabin. Anyway, I understand that the original log cabin had burned down and that previous owners had converted the granary into the house I lived in for the first ten years of my life. It doesn't sound quite as Abraham Lincoln-like to say I was born in a granary, does it?

This home had asphalt siding, cement floors, no insulation, drafty windows, no basement, one running faucet, a primitive light bulb hanging from each of the two main-floor rooms, a banging screen door, steep wooden stairs to the upstairs where a curtain and a makeshift wall divided my parents' room from the attic area where eventually all five of us children slept over the kitchen. We could see the bare rafters and roof boards above us as we went to sleep. In winter, we boys used to practice writing our alphabet letters with our fingernails in the frost on the roof boards.

Besides the one faucet and sink in the kitchen, there was an ice box, a wringer washing machine, a wood-burning kitchen stove with a hot water reservoir on the side, a tall cupboard system with perhaps eight doors, and a farmhouse kitchen table with wooden chairs. The kitchen was also the room where we bathed once a week in the laundry tubs. Our first chores were to stand on chairs at the sink to wash dishes and to carry wood from the wood pile to the kitchen stove.

The front room, as it was called, also had a wood-burning stove, a huge overstuffed used sofa (We called it the davenport.), an area carpet, and a couple rockers. Our luxury was a radio! Mostly I remember frightening music as we children were supposed to be falling asleep at night — music from "The Shadow Knows" or "The Green Hornet," but it also introduced me to country music, especially Hank Williams, Ernest Tubb, and The Grand Ole Opry.

With my parents' industrious determination and improvement in the post-war economy, a new house was built in 1951 just west of the old one. Much of the lumber for it was cut from our woods and sawn by Pa with a small sawmill he bought. Neighbors and relatives helped, but the home construction itself was left to hired carpenters. This new ranch-style house was magnificent! Imagine plastered walls, hardwood floors, arched doorways, a bay window in the living room, a dining room, a huge basement with a furnace, an attached garage, a refrigerator, a propane cooking range, built-in cupboards, and an indoor bathroom. This was luxury!

Farm life for me at that time offered the beauty of nature. Of course, there were always newborns — 500 new chicks every spring, kittens hidden in the hay mow a couple times a year and eventually proudly paraded out by their mothers, litters of pigs falling asleep while nursing, long-anticipated calves — sometimes twins — and sometimes born hidden in tall grass on the pasture, so hidden that we had to carefully observe the mother to be able to find the calf, chickens singing and sunning themselves and cackling their deliveries in the winter coop, the cow trails in the lane heading to the barn — even the flowers on weeds and bull thistles.

There were spectacular rainbows, sunrises, and sunsets without buildings obstructing the view. I'm sure that I saw "Ghost Riders in the Sky" when we played cowboys after supper. Although we weren't allowed outside during severe thunder and lightning storms, they were a wonder to watch. Rows of soybeans and corn just beginning to sprout, windrows of hay drying in the sun, huge snow drifts in winter, the woods changing color in the fall, "amber waves of grain," foggy summer mornings as we headed out to the pasture in bare feet through dewy grass to get the cows — all sights to admire.

Farm sounds were delightful — spring peepers, bullfrogs, and green frogs singing near the pasture ditch much of the early summer, two-month-old roosters learning to crow, pigeons cooing in the barn, a sow singing lullabies to her litter, rhythmic pulsing of milking machines, the barn radio with the country music of Hank Williams, Patsy Cline, and the Everly Brothers, our lead cow Judith's cowbell out in the summer pasture, company arriving up the gravel driveway, the cats' chorus as they anticipated their pan of milk every morning and evening, and the putt-putt of the one John Deere tractor we owned.

Even smells that might offend others became "sweet" smells to farm kids. Spreading manure on the fields was especially aromatic with clear distinctions as to whether we were cleaning the dairy barn, the pig house, or the chicken coop. The smell of fresh mown hay in the early summer and straw in mid-summer made us want to drive on country roads with the car windows down. Fermenting silage could be almost intoxicating.

Despite the beauty of farm life, I also learned the brutality of nature. We came to regard the beheading of dozens of chickens at a time, castrating of pigs, dehorning of cattle, tomcats killing whole litters of kittens, cows with foot rot, mastitis, and bloat, baby pigs killed by their mothers' carelessly lying on them or even their eating them, aborted calf fetuses, catching frogs and chopping off their legs for supper, cows with tender backs as fly larvae burst forth, baby pigs with painful joints, cats with distemper, baby chicks threatened by chicken hawks, cows with breach births requiring help with the fence stretcher, possums, raccoons, and foxes raiding the chicken coup sometimes leaving a dozen dead, lightning storms that ignited barn fires and destroyed trapped livestock and on one occasion killed a cow that was hit by lightning while standing under an oak tree, chickens killed by passing cars on the road, cats' legs amputated as they hid in the hay field where they thought they were out of reach of the hay mower, calves separated from their mothers within days of birth leaving the cows bawling in mourning for a week or more, Future Farmers of America pest hunts (five cents per sparrow head and mouse tail; ten-cents per pigeon head and rat tail), whole sections of newly planted fields flooded or frozen in early spring, sections of fields trampled and devoured when the cattle occasionally got through an open gate or through a broken fence — all these things became a normal part of life for a farm kid.

Farm accidents, sometimes fatal, were common — the kinds of accidents that weren't so likely among city dwellers — falling from a silo and landing on the edge of a wagon rack, getting clothing or limbs caught in moving farm machinery, broken bones and bruises caused by cattle, injuries while playing on or repairing farm machinery, fingers cut in buzz saws, falls from farm machinery, ax accidents while splitting wood or hand injuries while repairing barbed wire fences.

Farm life taught me to tolerate discomfort. On long, hot summer days, we always had a huge thermos of water with us as we baled hay, combined wheat, or cultivated corn for six or more hours at a stretch. Ma brought refills for the water jug when she could. Back in the '50s, a good tan was still considered healthy; unfortunately, long days on a hay wagon or on a tractor cultivating corn or disking a field back and forth for hours without shirts often resulted in sunburn. We had to wear heavy gloves in hot weather while baling hay, and the knees of our jeans wore thin from boosting forty-pound bales over our heads as we stacked them on an ever bumpy, jiggling wagon.

Our Christmas school break was focused on cutting our winter's supply of firewood. Using the tractor, Pa had usually piled lots of logs and branches from fallen trees in the woods and had the buzz saw and wagons ready for the day school got out. After fall harvest, there wasn't much hard work besides routine chores, so after that first day of cutting firewood, our muscles were so sore we could hardly move. Pa's solution was that we should get back out there the next day and loosen them up. Unfortunately, he was right. Our winter coats, hats, and gloves were not insulated. The coats had buttons rather than zippers, and the cotton gloves had holes and were soaked from handling snow-covered branches. Long underwear and constant movement helped keep us warm, but our hands, ears, and toes suffered. After the wood was cut and hauled by wagon to the house, it had to be pitched into the basement through a small "coal" door and stacked in the large furnace room. Back in school in January, I got to hear stories of what fun the town kids had during their Christmas break.

Rock picking was another back breaker. I think my sisters even got in on that "fun." Pa usually chose days for that job when, as he would say, "My back went out last night." Consequently, he was the designated tractor driver slowly pulling a sturdy stoneboat, as we called it, on skids across barren soil. From his tractor seat, he could of course point out rocks and stones we might have otherwise overlooked — sometimes deliberately? Occasionally, we'd have to dig a stone loose, and sometimes it took all of us to roll one to the stoneboat and umph it on. Naturally, the job was only half done when the stoneboat was full. It had to be unloaded, sometimes near a fence row; other times near farm buildings where the stones would be used in future construction of some sort.

In my youngest years and before I was old enough to help much with haying, we put up loose hay much as the Amish still do. That required a system of forks, pullies, and ropes to move the hay from the wagon into the barn. My only part in that was to pull the slack ropes back and forth. For a number of years in my early teens, we harvested chopped hay. A chopper pulled behind the tractor blew the dry, chopped hay into a wagon box. Pa had put hoists under the wagon beds, so when we unloaded the hay into a conveyor that moved the hay to a blower that blew it into the mow, our only job was to use long-handled, hooked forks to drag the hay out of the back of the hoisted rack into the conveyor. Imagine the chaff times ten! It was all over our faces, in our hair, down our shirts, in our shoes, and in our throats and noses. We wore cowboy kerchiefs and later what looked a little like surgical masks, but still our rag handkerchiefs turned black for days thereafter whenever we blew our noses. It seems strange to say that baling hay, in contrast, was almost a pleasure.

Harvesting wheat and oats was a chaff-choking, back-breaking job. In my earliest years of helping with that, the combine had a bagger, so as the machine thrashed the wheat, it was collected in fifty-to-eighty-pound bags which were periodically loaded onto a wagon and later stored in a granary. Lots of lifting! Later, the loose wheat was simply augured from a bin on the combine into a wagon; then with heavy scoop shovels, we pitched it from the wagon into a bin for storage. More chaffy heavy lifting! Eventually, the wagons had hoists so that the oats or wheat poured out a small door at the back of the wagon into an augur that moved it into the storage bin. As the bin filled, someone needed to move the wheat away from the augur so that it wouldn't back up and plug. There was very little space between the top of the bin and the roof, too little to effectively use a shovel, so trying as hard as we could with our hands to keep up with the augur, we sweated in the chaff, bumped our heads, and probably swore at those unloading the wagon to slow down. The wheat was stored under government contract until the next summer. It had to pass inspections for mold, mice contamination, and insect infestation, etc. To reduce this contamination, we were allowed to use a liquid chemical which was poured over the filled bin. Remember, the filled bin left very little space between the wheat and the roof. We used gallon tins of the liquid, and as we poured it on the wheat, we had to bend over so close to the wheat that we could only try to hold our breath long enough to not breathe the chemicals. That never worked. I remember once passing out for a short time.

Part of the discomfort I learned to tolerate was the fact that I was a farm kid in a predominately town school. When we were old enough to help with some everyday chores — usually at ten years old — we got up about 6:00 every day. With Pa and all three of us boys helping, we could finish the feeding, milking, and cleaning up in the barn, pigpen, and chicken coop in about an hour. That left us about an hour more for breakfast, changing clothes, and packing for school before the bus arrived. We always ate breakfast together at the table. It wasn't a matter of carrying food around the house as we got ready. By this time, we lived in our new house with one bathroom, and my sisters seemed to need more than their share of time in there. Our house was always the first stop for the school bus because we lived the farthest from the school — about seven miles by direct route, at least double that with trips down almost every country road. The ride to school was about forty-five minutes. Naturally, we were also the last off the bus in the afternoon.

We had our farm clothes and our school clothes. In my elementary years before I helped with chores, I wore the same clothes all week. In junior high and high school, we had about a half hour after breakfast to get changed and cleaned up. I know that sometimes my hair didn't have all the chaff out of it; other times, my teeth didn't get brushed, and at least one memorable day, I recall sitting in class with a little manure on my farm shoes — the only shoes I had. My nails were often dirty and my hands chapped. I'm glad I wasn't the students who had to sit near me.

We always carried our lunches. In elementary school, my brothers and I used small Farmer Peet lard buckets for lunch boxes and envied the fancy Howdy Doody, Roy Rodgers, and Superman lunch boxes town kids carried. Lunch was always a sandwich (usually peanut butter, tuna, or bologna), leftover dessert (cookies, cake, or a rolled-up cold pancake with cinnamon and sugar sprinkled inside), and a small thermos of milk. Until I was in junior high, Ma made homemade bread. Then she started working at a family-owned grocery in Owosso, and we started to have store-bought bread. The problem was, as I saw it as an eight-year-old, Ma's homemade bread wasn't nearly as pretty and tasty-looking as the town kids' Wonder Bread. Thus, I shamefully hid my sandwich in its wax paper and tried to eat behind my lard pale lunch bucket.

Sports and most extracurricular activities were after school or in the evenings. After school for us was always chore time — pitching silage out of the silo, getting hay down from the mows, cleaning manure out of the gutters, carrying water to the chickens, putting straw down for the cattle, milking, and cleaning the milking equipment. Until Dave got a car when he was sixteen, attending football and basketball games and school plays and dances was out of the question.

Farm life taught us to show up on time, to be reliable, to do our part, that the farm animals must eat before we had meals, and that we didn't quit until the work was done. It also taught us generosity and cooperation. In my young years during and after World War II, most farmers couldn't afford the machinery that they later went heavily into debt to own; furthermore, thrashing machines and silo filling equipment weren't being produced on a large enough scale for every farmer to own one. I recall days when the thrashing and silo filling crews spent several days at our farm each year. One man was the owner of the equipment, and he might have had a couple hired men to help, but the crew of twelve or fifteen included all the nearby neighbor men and boys as well. As soon as they finished at our place, they moved to the next farm, and Pa went with them. It didn't seem to matter that some farms may have needed four days work while others needed only two. The only pay other than that to the owner of the equipment was that neighbors helped each other. That and huge dinner meals at noon. I recall long makeshift tables set outside on sawhorses. Ma pretty much prepared these meals on her own — always lots of potatoes and gravy, pork chops or chicken or beef roast, green beans or sweet corn or cabbage. And always dessert — cake or pies or cookies. I think neighbor women or Grandma Demerly might have sent a pie or cake now and then, but it was mostly Ma's work at the wood-burning stove while looking after us five kids. Naturally, most of the clean-up work was hers too though she taught us boys to wash dishes long before we could do farm chores. These "harvest bees" continued even after every farmer had appropriate equipment to do his own harvesting. Such was always the case when a farmer was sick or hospitalized. Other farmers teamed up to get his crops in or milk his cows until he recovered.

During the winter months to supplement the farm income in my early years, Pa worked at the Oldsmobile factory in Lansing. He rode to the night shift with Rudy Kozumplik who lived across the road from us. In the '50s when Ma and we boys could handle the chores, Pa hauled mobile homes from the factory in Marlette to destinations as far away as Kansas and Missouri. If it was a short day trip to Ohio or

Indiana or within Michigan, he occasionally took one of us along with him. I remember riding with him only once. It seemed truly strange to have his attention all to myself. Though we didn't talk much, he helped me understand how to read the map and road signs, how to estimate distances and time to the next town, and what to anticipate ahead of us. I particularly recall having lunch at a truck stop. I was probably twelve at the time and had never been in a restaurant. Pa showed me the menu, but he ordered for both of us. I don't remember what I ate there except for this strange stuff he called "cold slaw." At home, we had cabbage, but I had never heard of "cold slaw. Now I understand that he said "cole" but having never heard that word, I guessed that he had said "cold".

Because friends and even neighbors were too far away to visit frequently, we developed a family bond and depended on that for our primary social contact. Until Ma took a job at a family grocery when all of us kids were out of elementary school, our parents didn't "go to work." They were almost always at home though that could have been some distance away in a field. Except for school days, we had three meals a day together around a table large enough for all seven of us. By the early 1950s, we had our first television which received two channels. At first, shows were televised from about 4:00 in the afternoon until 10:00 at night. We all watched the same shows — ones my parents chose. After school for a while before starting our chores, there were Art Linkletter, Kate Smith, and American Bandstand. After supper, we watched the news for a half hour. My earliest memories of television news included reports on the Korean War. Then in the evening it was *You Bet Your Life*, *The Honeymooners*, *I Love Lucy*, and entertainment by Milton Berle, Ed Sullivan, Jack Benny, Arthur Godfrey, Lawrence Welk, Perry Como, and Dinah Shore — all primarily it seems to me today, a venue to sell cigarettes, cars, appliances, cosmetics, beer, shaving necessities, and TV dinners — consumerism at its best.

Other than routine chores, Sundays were for relaxation unless weather dictated getting a crop in before rain. While we children were in church and Sunday school, Ma prepared the usual big Sunday dinner while Pa worked in his shop and read the Sunday *Detroit Free Press* in peace without five children in the house. Perhaps he even meditated and gave thanks for this blessing. Sunday dinner was served at noon. Almost all businesses, even grocery stores, were closed on Sundays. Sometimes relatives or neighbors dropped in without notice — just to visit for a couple hours. They seldom brought children, but we children sat listening to adult conversation without interruptions. Nothing could match the luxury of a long Sunday afternoon nap. Occasionally, we visited neighbors or relatives on Sunday afternoons. When we returned, Pa could always tell whether someone had stopped to visit us by tire tracks that weren't our own in the gravel driveway, and he claimed to recognize whose tracks they were. Since the house doors were never locked (I'm not sure we even had a key), it wasn't unusual to find a note from visitors on the kitchen table.

Our social life as teenagers was mostly school and church activities. Until Dave got a car, we never went to plays, dances, or sports events at school in the evenings. Even then, we went only if he wanted to drag us along, so our social contact and friendships were within the context of our classrooms, study hall, lunchtime, and pep assemblies. We boys never had friends stay at our home overnight though in later years, our sisters had pajama parties. Thus, our friendships with schoolmates was relatively superficial. Dave's interest in church activities began to wane after he had a car and new freedom. Nevertheless, the rest of us went to church several times a week for regular church services and Sunday School, for choir practice, and for Methodist Youth Fellowship meetings. The small country church was two miles from home, so our primary friendships developed among farm kids within the farming community. Still, we saw them only at church activities.

I don't remember either of my grandfathers who both died when I was very young. My maternal grandmother lived in Idaho with her oldest son, so I didn't know her either. Grandma Demerly, however, left an indelible, but unfortunately, not happy memory for all of us. My mother says she was a wonderfully kind, affable, and generous woman, but the memories of my siblings and me would contest that. She passed away when I was nine. She lived with her daughter about three miles from us, but she was our babysitter when both of our parents were away. Ma and Pa took a western trip to visit Pa's cousin in Wyoming and another to Florida when we were all young. Grandma, who was in her late 60s and who had raised six children of her own, wasn't about to put up with any nonsense from five little ones all born within seven years. She kept us terrified by threatening to come upstairs with the pancake flopper if we didn't "pipe down" at nap time.

Other times if we were a little rowdy, she'd tell us to go get a switch off the "willer tree." In fact, she never had to use the pancake flopper or the switch. Perhaps the only fond memory I have of her is watching her in her apron seated on a kitchen chair peeling apples. Amazingly, she could peel a whole apple with one slice. She gathered us seated on the floor in front of her and fed us baby birds these apple peeling worms.

I had twenty-nine cousins, but I hardly knew any of them except the Graves, my mother's sister's three kids who were about our ages. More than half of these cousins I never met but once or twice at most. Because Pa was a late-in-life child, most of his brothers' and sister's children were adults when I was a child. Ma's older brother, Uncle Roger, had five children the same age as we were, but they lived in California. They visited Michigan for a few days and were with us the day that Marilyn Monroe died on August 5, 1962. I visited them in San Jose a number of times while I was in the Army. Ma's younger brother, Uncle Lynn, adopted a son after I left home.

Pa's sister, Aunt Leora, who lived nearby had two sons. Lee was about three years older than Dave; Bruce was younger than Sal. My only clear memory of Lee was that he introduced all three of us boys to cigarettes when I was six or seven years old. We were hiding in his barn — what a place to be playing with matches! — when he lit up and offered each of us a puff or two. Of course, we all gagged and choked, and for me, that was the last cigarette I smoked. Thank you, Lee.

For a number of years, we held a Demerly Sunday summer picnic reunion at McCurdy Park in Corunna, a few miles from Owosso. All of Pa's family came including some old aunts and a cousin whom I'd only heard about, so I did have a vague acquaintance with them. Uncle Clyde was the postmaster in Clawson, Michigan. I think he was the only one of his siblings to finish high school. It was curious for me that during these reunions, he stood near his car listening to the Tigers' game on the car radio, something we never did on the farm.

Aunt Vivian, Ma's sister, lived in Jackson, Michigan, and had three children who spent time on the farm with us in summers. Scott was my age, so he could help with chores with our careful supervision. For him, what we thought was work, he thought was fun. We had to train him not to startle the cattle or get his bare feet stepped on by them. He did make chores fun for a while. Pa had made an electric-powered lawn-mower which took at least three of us to operate on our huge sloping lawn — one pushing, one pulling with an attached rope, and one carrying the long electric cord. It seemed like the lawn was never mown. As soon as we finished, we needed to start again. While Scott was helping us mow, he somehow managed to get his toes under the mower which sliced through his shoe and cut a couple of his toes quite badly. Ma, who always seemed to know just how to handle these emergencies, got the bleeding stopped with cold rags, bandaged his foot, and took him to the doctor feeling very bad that this should happen to her nephew on her watch.

In my isolation and perhaps as a reflection of the 1950s in general, I knew little about weddings, pregnancy, divorce, and funerals. I was in college but living at home when I first attended a wedding, that of one of our church youth friends at the local church. I was five years old when my youngest sibling was born. I remember Ma using Sal's arrival date as a tool to try to teach me time on the clock and calendar whenever I asked when the baby was coming. One of the women at church became pregnant in my high school years, but women wore what we called blossom blouses to try to disguise their pregnancy, and nobody seemed to talk about pregnancy in public. Several of my high school classmates became pregnant before graduation and left school. Little was heard from or about them thereafter. Divorce too was not discussed publicly. In fact, I didn't realize until my teen years that my aunts — Vivian and Leora — had been divorced and remarried even though they had sons with last names different from their current married names. Nobody talked about divorce, and few couples divorced. Children did not attend funerals. Strangely, my father's funeral when I was thirty-one years old, was the first one I attended.

We rarely went into Owosso or neighboring towns. On a few occasions, I recall trips to the A&P grocery, but we had to remain in the car while Ma did the shopping. Imagine that today! We never went to dentists, doctors (except for dire emergencies), or barbers. Pa pulled our teeth with a pair of pliers. The tooth fairy brought a dime for each tooth---a dime with Winged Mercury, which I imagined was the tooth fairy himself in flight. Ma cut our hair with scissors and manual clippers which forever pinched and pulled. She'd tell us to sit still, but how was that possible? As teenagers, when we began to save a little money, we did begin Christmas shopping in town for our siblings and parents. That could be completed with one trip.

One of the local farm women initiated a 4-H club in our area. I'm not sure how we boys found ourselves as part of it, but we became active 4-H-ers, both in dairy and photography. Once again, our "friends" were local farm boys whom we knew only through 4-H. We met monthly and learned how to make rope halters for our cattle and how to train and groom them for showing at the annual county fair. We were also taught how to keep records of the cost of their feed and veterinarian expenses. Pa gave each of us boys a newborn heifer when we joined 4-H; we named them Molly, Hazel, and Phyllis. Naturally, through our high school years, they became cows with their own calves. We were taught how to weigh and record the amount of milk from each of our cows so that when the bi-monthly farm milk check arrived, we could determine our portion of the profits. During the week-long Shiawassee County Fair, a few 4-H members took turns staying at a bunk house overnight in order to look after the animals. I think my turn came one night when I was a sophomore in high school. Before then, I had never stayed overnight away from my family. It wasn't a very restful night.

We boys were also members of the Future Farmers of America (FFA), a high school organization for farm boys and now girls. My personal project was raising pigs. Prior to that, we did occasionally raise a pig or two, but my project grew from two duroc piglets named Tutti and Frutti (the result of the influence of the music of Little Richard and Pat Boone) to about forty pigs by the time I went to college. Of course, many were marketed along the way. Although

I learned some skills about raising pigs from books and class lessons, most of my learning was hands-on, trial and error. Pa helped by building a nearly-pig-proof fence around a three-acre field and acquiring an old box container that had been part of a delivery truck, which became the pig house until I built one in farm shop from lumber we had sawn from our woods. I was really nervous the night Frutti went into labor with her first litter. She must have been nervous as well. I had built a crate in the box container according to directions to prevent her from accidentally lying on the piglets. I ran an extension cord from the barn to a heat lamp in the pig house, and I sat up all night watching over the delivery of eight babies. I think I was allowed to skip school the next day. With this experimental litter, I learned to vaccinate, castrate, ween, feed, water, build a shade structure, make a mud hole, market — and love these pigs.

I was the president and secretary of the FFA, part of a parliamentary procedure competitive team, and a not-very-successful competitor in public speaking. In my junior year, I was selected to go in spring to a long-weekend FFA leadership training camp at Higgins Lake, about 100 miles from home. Other than an overnight at the county fair, I had never been away from my family overnight. My first challenge was to convince Pa to let me go, to miss chores for three days. My worry was much greater than it needed to be, but I was never comfortable speaking personally with him. Off I went with the agricultural teacher. We arrived in the early afternoon and had meetings. Supper was at sunset that day, and as we took our places at long tables, I was suddenly struck with homesickness, desperate homesickness. I longed to be home. I could hardly eat. I imagined my family together at home. I wanted to cry but couldn't in front of all these other boys who seemed to be having a wonderful time. As soon as possible, I found my way to my bunk and probably sobbed myself silently to sleep. I was preoccupied enough with sessions to get over that initial grief, but counted the hours till I could get home.

Since there were no neighborhood kids down the alley to teach us "kick the can" or other urban games, we created fun when we had free time from chores — things like apple fights, a game we called raggy-baggy (sort of our version of rugby before we had ever heard of rugby), ghost game (a version of hide-and-go-seek played in the dark) standing under the barn's downspouts during rain storms, playing traffic cop and school bus with our one scooter and bike, digging holes in the dirt under the apple trees where we played with our farm toys and trucks, sliding and ice skating on a small farm pond, sledding down the driveway and quite often running into the farm lane barbed wire fence, playing fox and goose while waiting for the school bus, trading comic books with our Graves cousins, the Rundells, and the Shippees, playing cement mixer in our bare feet in mud puddles, swinging on ropes fastened to the track in the peak of the barn, and making forts and tunnels with hay bales. In winter and on rainy days when we didn't have outside work to do, we colored in coloring books or played with our dolls, train sets, toy farms, and toy ranch sets. We had a favorite set of "brown blocks" — children's construction blocks that had been my mother's, some dominoes, Pick-up Sticks, Old Maid cards, checkers, Uncle Wriggly (a board game that had been Ma's), paper airplanes, and rubber band spitball fights (only when Pa wasn't in the house). In our teens, we played cards with our parents, usually euchre or canasta or a game called Pedro.

In our teen years when we were all committed to daily farm chores and extra work during harvesting of hay, wheat, oats, corn, straw, and even field stones, at the end of hot chaffy days, we'd all pile into the car, usually a Ford, and go to Round Lake in Laingsburg to rinse off. None of us could swim. Ma and Pa usually sat in the car listening to Hank Williams and Patsy Cline. On a few occasions, we took picnic supplies and drove to a park in Owosso or to a roadside park on M-21. Sometimes we drove to Perry for ice cream. Before television, we'd go to Morrice on summer Saturday nights to watch the free show projected on a wooden screen. We sat on outdoor wooden benches and watched Gene Autry, Lash Larue, Hopalong Cassidy, Roy Rodgers, and Abbott and Costello — food for our imaginary cowboys and Indians games.

The local stock car races at the Owosso Speedway and the annual Shiawassee County Fair were special events. Pa loved machinery and cars, so the stock car races were a special attraction. He knew a couple of the drivers. Children under ten were admitted free, but I recall passing for under ten when I was fourteen. I was a runt anyway, but on bent knees, I was especially short. I was fascinated by the colorful cars and the fancy shirts and the checkered flags. The demolition derby was sort of our version of watching a video game, I guess. I imagined myself as a race car driver. Maybe my wife, Martha, thinks I still have that thought as I "speed" down the freeway. Pa attended the county fair only to examine the new farm machinery and to talk business with the exhibitors. We were not allowed to run off by ourselves; instead, we moped bored and listened to all the fun other people were having on the carnival rides. I longed to go through the animal barns and the home exhibits with baked goods and hobby projects. Once or twice, we attended horse pulling and tractor pulling events and one country western stage show. As we became teens with our 4-H cattle, we were able to wander wherever time allowed, but I don't recall ever having the nerve to pay to see the two-headed calf, the bearded lady, the tattooed man, the Siamese twins, or the 600-pound lady.

After an outdoor drive-in theater opened in Owosso in the early '50s, we started going to the movies a few times during the summer. I had never gone to an indoor theater. There were usually previews of coming attractions, a cartoon or two, a first film followed by intermission with advertising and concession stand invitations, and finally, the second film. Seldom did we stay awake through the second film. Ma usually packed snacks for us, and if we had to use the restrooms, we all had to go at the same time to look out for one another.

When we children ranged from ages seven to fourteen more or less, our parents bought a used 1940s travel trailer/camper. Pa put considerable work into remodeling it so that it could accommodate the whole family. He resided and painted it, fit in a bunk bed over the main bed in the rear of the trailer, fashioned the table in the booth eating arrangement in a way that the table could be placed between the facing bench seats to create another bed Thus, with one or two of us sleeping on the floor, our family of seven was ready to travel in luxury. And so began our journeys into the outside world between planting and harvesting. Mostly we took three-or-four-day trips to state parks while a neighbor looked after the farm animals. I particularly remember a stay at Pentwater State Park on Lake Michigan's shore. We loved the sand dunes and beach and gentle waves, but the blistering sunburn was a painful souvenir. While camping at Mackinaw State Park, we watched construction of the bridge. Years later with my own children, we spent much of our summers in a tent at these same parks.

After we boys were old enough to stay home to do the chores by ourselves while the others camped, we took turns, two of us at a time, doing chore duties. Just to keep us busy, Pa always found extra jobs that he expected to be finished by the time the campers returned. Maybe it was sweeping all the cobwebs out of the dairy barn or cleaning the bull pen or chopping the weeds along the electric pasture fence. After being left behind a time or two, we started to prefer home duty and its limited freedom, but we had to pretend that we missed the camping trips. By then, Dave had his driver's license, so using the farm pick-up or his car or even the big farm truck, we could sneak away. Usually, we tried to get all the extra work done the first day just in case the travelers came home early. Maybe we'd do the milking a little early or a little late. We could eat whatever we could prepare whenever we wanted. Once we took the big farm truck and drove to Laingsburg to listen to jukebox hits, drink Cokes, and play pinball machines with a couple farm friends. On the way home on a deserted country road, Dave missed a turn, and we wound up in a shallow ditch and couldn't push the truck out of it. We were about three miles from home and didn't know any of the local farmers. Besides that, we didn't want to be found out. That kind of news spreads fast in a farm community. Two of us stayed with the truck and two others started home on foot to get chains and a tractor. With luck, we did get the truck back on the road, and if Pa ever learned of it, he never told us. Do you suppose he would have been proud of the way we handled the emergency?

My first true view of the rest of the world was a trip to Florida in this trailer during Christmas break. I was in tenth grade and excelled in geography, so passing every state line on two-lane highways (before I-75) was a milestone. Winding our way through the Smoky Mountains on treacherously narrow curving roads hauling a trailer was an amusement ride in itself. As we passed poor Appalachian farms, Pa tried to convince us that cows grazing on the hillside had two shorter legs on one side so that they wouldn't fall off the mountain. In Georgia, we saw signs of segregation at gas stations with "Whites Only" signs on the restrooms and drinking fountains. As we approached Florida, I kept watching for the first palm tree. Florida was truly another world. We visited an alligator farm, orange and grapefruit groves, a water-skiing exhibition, and tropical gardens near Orlando (before Disney moved in). We traveled through the Everglades and partway down the Keys. This wasn't Michigan!

As farm kids, and probably true of many city kids in the 1940s and '50s when the average family was three or more children, we learned postponed gratification, in other words, patience. Days passed at a pace determined by our parents. Bed time was inflexible. Meals were eaten after chores were done. Pa always said that we wouldn't be fed until after the animals were. We learned it was futile to ask for new clothes or toys except for Christmas when Ma put out the Penney's and Ward's catalogues in December and said we could pick out one toy we thought we'd like and maybe we'd get it. We never got birthday gifts, but Ma did allow us to choose the kind of birthday cake we preferred. On Christmas morning, we weren't allowed to snoop or touch the gifts. We only looked at a distance and went about our usual chores. To reinforce our ability to remain patient, our parents started a tradition that on Christmas morning, we had to eat as many pancakes as we were years old. That prolonged breakfast. Fortunately, the pancakes began to diminish in size as we got into our teens. Inevitably, Pa found an extra hour or two-hour-long chore that just had to be taken care of on Christmas morning while the girls had to help Ma start a big noon meal. Even after that, Pa generally had something to do in his shop before we could get to the presents. Rarely did we open gifts before 11:00.

Another way our patience was reinforced was in the purchase of our first (and only) bike. That finally occurred when I was about twelve. None of us had learned how to ride a bike yet. My parents had planted about an acre of pickles every summer for several summers. Pickle picking is something all five of us could do by then. Granted, we boys could go at it more ambitiously than our sisters, but we all did what we could. We earned five cents per milk bucket of pickles, dumped them into burlap grain sacks, and stuffed the sacks into the car trunk. Almost daily when the pickles were being harvested, Ma drove them to the pickle processing plant in Laingsburg. You might ask, "How many pickles could a pickle processing plant process if ...?" The answer is "tons." With great patience and annual calculations, we realized about three years later that we had accumulated enough savings to afford the beautiful full-sized boy's bike exhibited in the Ward's window in Owosso. We had to negotiate what color to get, red or blue. Of course, it was too big for most of us, but like our shoes and shirts, we were expected to grow into it, and it was expected to last forever. Dave learned to ride it quite soon without too many spills on the gravel driveway. Every spill required a careful inspection to see if there were scratches or dents. Eventually, Dick and I could also handle it. The girls sometimes just walked the bike around to get their turns. That bike did outlast five childhoods! If all of us wanted to go to a neighbor's house at the same time, like circus acrobats and naturally without any safety gear, we all got on the bike and went — one on the peddles, one seated on the bar, one on the seat, one the handlebars, and one on the rear fender.

We seldom helped ourselves to snacks. We waited until mealtime, and we ate what was served — like it or not. For us on the farm, there were always milk and eggs, beef, pork, and chicken, and standard vegetables such as potatoes, green beans, navy beans, stewed tomatoes, onions, canned corn, beets, and cabbage, but never asparagus. Pa had worked as a hired man on a farm that produced asparagus, and during the six weeks that it was in season and needed cutting all day every day, the housewife served it in one form or another day after day. Pa said that harvesting it and eating it for nearly two months a year was enough for a lifetime for him. Many of the vegetables were ones Ma had canned from our garden or from vegetables neighbors had given us. We had macaroni, but not spaghetti. The big meal, we called it dinner, was served at noon when we weren't in school. Supper was usually a variation of leftovers. Breakfasts were pancakes, toast, eggs, sausage, bacon, or oatmeal. The toaster was an old electric one with handles to manually flip the toast when it was sufficiently burned on one side. We took turns watching it, and if a piece got blackened on our watch, that was our piece to eat. We rarely had fruit except for strawberries and apples in the summer. After Ma began work at the grocery, we were introduced to cereal — Grape-Nuts, corn flakes, Rice Krispies, shredded wheat, bran flakes. Quite often the boxes had puzzles, jokes, riddles, etc. printed on the back for our amusement as we ate our breakfast. Even better, some had a small prize in the box — a plastic ring, a sheriff's badge, a colored picture of a bird or dog or wild animal. Many had mail-in offers with so many box tops — things like a plastic airplane, a glow-in-the-dark belt, a magic trick, a book to paste the colored pictures in. What excitement to receive mail addressed to us!

At meals, Pa sat at the head of the table with Ma on the corner at his right. The girls sat to Ma's right, and we boys filled in the remaining seats according to whoever got to the table first. Pa was always served first, and dishes were passed clockwise around the table, so there was some advantage to sitting next to Pa. By the time the dish reached Ma, it often looked like scraps or leftovers, but she never complained. We children learned not to talk at the table. "Children are to be seen, not heard." We did not say grace before meals; however, we were expected to say, "Please pass the potatoes." I'm sure my parents wanted relative solitude rather than five children conversing, squabbling, horsing around, whining.... Instead, we listened to our parents' conversation, usually about daily events, the weather (important to farmers), neighbors, plans for the day, etc. Generally, the radio was turned on to the local Owosso station, WOAP, for the farm report, Polka Party on Sunday at noon, popular and country music, local news and weather, and sometimes a soap opera. We learned to help ourselves to some of everything, like it or not, and to finish our plate before we could be excused. That took some real effort on my part whenever liver was the main dish. Our parents drank coffee and sometimes tea, never alcohol. When Pa's coffee cup was empty, he'd gently rattle it on the saucer or say, "More java?" We drank milk at every meal, never soda (or pop as Midwesterners called it). In our early years, we had narrow, colored plastic glasses that someone had given us. They seemed very unstable in the small hands of an eight-year-old, so inevitably there was a spill from time to time, and naturally, the spill was always in the direction of Pa. In an effort to put an end to that, Pa ordered that anyone who spilled milk had to leave the table and stand facing the kitchen with his back to the table until the rest of the family was finished eating. Then the culprit could finish his cold dinner alone. I can't say that it eliminated accidents despite our caution. On one occasion while I was the "stand-alone", I recall imagining Hopalong Cassidy, one of my cowboy movie heroes, barging through the kitchen door and ordering Pa to let us sit down and eat. Hopalong let me down.

Even as teenagers, we rarely contributed to conversation at the table. Our opinions were insignificant. There were never queries from our parents about what we did at school. The one most memorable suppertime for me occurred when I was a senior in high school. Dave was home on leave after sixteen weeks of basic training in the Army. That evening was stunningly remarkable! Pa talked to and listened to Dave in the way he talked to adult company! Dave was no longer just his "oldest boy."

Once when we were teenagers, Ma overheard us grumbling about "the same old thing" for supper, so she asked what we'd prefer. It was unanimous — dessert! As it was, we did have dessert after most dinners and suppers — cake, pie, or cookies — but apparently it didn't seem like much to us at the time. Starting the next morning, we had a luscious chocolate cake while our parents had bacon, eggs, and toast. Even in our lunch bags — cookies only. For supper it was apple pie as Ma and Pa helped themselves to meatloaf and mashed potatoes. In less than a week, we surrendered and quit our grumbling.

On another occasion when Chef Boyardee boxed pizza was becoming popular, Ma noticed how often customers were buying it and asked how they liked it. They did. She thought she'd try it for a surprise and something a little different. As Pa and we boys came into the house for supper after doing the chores, he *was* surprised! "What is that stink?" he proclaimed. "It's pizza. All the customers at the store said it's fantastic, so I thought I'd try it," Ma replied. Do you suppose a meat-and-potatoes guy was about to try that? Pa had a hamburger while the rest of us nibbled at the pizza, which in reality, wasn't very good, but it was certainly something different.

No doubt, farm life in the 1940s and '50s influenced the person I have become. I certainly learned elements of responsibility, teamwork, self-reliance, patience (some might say stubbornness), appreciation for natural beauty, determination, and humility. I learned how to take initiative and face hardships. At the same time, in young adulthood, I lacked social skills in a wider world. I was reclusive, naïve, and academically unprepared for college work. Improvement in those areas took years of experience.

3

Being Schooled, Part I

Although Ma read to us and taught us numbers, colors, and shapes in our preschool years, when I started kindergarten in 1945, most parents in our rural school district seemed to rely on the teachers to take care of all that. I had my older brother to show me the way around, to get me to my classroom, and to get me on the red-white-and-blue school bus for home. Kindergarten for me was all day though we took naps on our own small carpets after lunch.

From kindergarten to eleventh grade, I attended classes in Perry's one school building — a brick, slate-roofed, two-storied, wood-floored building which was built in 1902. An old wooden one-room school house had been moved next to the brick building to offer extra space. It is in this building where I attended kindergarten and years later had choral music, biology, and agricultural classes. Within a few years after I was enrolled, the post-war baby boom began to demand more room. A four-room addition was built to accommodate kindergarten through third grade. One year, my younger brother, Dick, and I were in the same "overflow" classroom. I was placed there with four or five other "accelerated" third graders with the thought that the second-grade teacher, in the manner of the many one-room country schools in Shiawassee County, could teach both levels.

As the population increased and additional one-room schools were annexed to Perry Rural Consolidated Schools, classes were held in hallways, on the school stage, in the library, and on the gym floor. The corridors and the one broad stairway became very congested while students passed between classes in high school.

Three memories from Mrs. Reynolds' fourth grade stand out. I was awarded with a little certificate for "perfect posture," probably the result of Ma's forever reminding me to "sit up." Students were called to the board to work out arithmetic problems to determine who could most quickly and accurately solve problems. I was *not* the winner in these embarrassing challenges. In fact, I was still working on most problems after all the other contestants had turned to face the class. Geography classes disoriented me for life. Mrs. Reynolds' wall map was mounted on the south wall, but whenever she pointed to the map indicating that the top of the map was "north," I understood that that direction was north. Despite my military orientation and map reading training and my world travels, to this day, whenever I am in the Owosso/Perry area, I have to cautiously recall my directions, usually by remembering that some farm land that Ma and Pa bought joined our property to the east and was referred to as the East Place. I remember first watching an educational film in this class, a black-and-white piece on postwar Europe in its desolate state struggling to reconstruct. Even though my family was living in near poverty at that time, I felt very privileged after watching that film.

Mrs. Bruno's fifth grade was on the main floor with windows facing the playground. Her son, Dexter, was in fourth grade at the time. She could see him on the playground, and if she didn't like what she saw in his behavior, she opened the window and yelled, "Dexter!" That seemed to resolve the issue. We had a student named Harold who I now realize was probably mentally disabled and had failed a couple classes. He was old enough to start shaving. He was seated in the front row near the teacher's desk so that whenever he started giggling inappropriately or making interruptive comments, she could easily wallop him on the head with the dictionary.

I especially enjoyed Mrs. Peck's sixth-grade class. We painted wall murals on huge rolls of butcher paper depicting the changing of the seasons; we made Christmas cards for our parents with black and white photos that Mrs. Peck had taken of each student standing in front of a neighbor's snow-covered spruce tree; we had spelling, history, and geography bees where — in great contrast to picking ball teams at recess — everybody wanted me on his/her team and where I was often the last "man" standing, unlike my performance during math drills in fourth grade. One student named Carol was epileptic. Every week or two, she had a seizure during class time. The teacher hurried to help her lie on the floor where she convulsed for a few minutes while we watched stunned even after we had witnessed these episodes a number of times. Students seated near her gradually learned to detect signs that Carol was about to have a seizure. When she recovered, she sat up dazed and incoherent and then always very embarrassed. She was helped to her chair, and class went on. Sixth grade was also the year I had frequent unpredictable nose bleeds. What a mess that was! I always had a rag handkerchief in my pocket, but that was only a temporary solution. The teacher sometimes sent another student to get cold wet paper towels, and if I sat for a while with my head back with these wet towels over my nose, the bleeding eventually stopped.

My elementary school years also included experimental fluoride dental treatments at the county seat in Corunna and with parental permission, polio vaccinations. At the end of the school year, the upper elementary students were bussed for the day to Potter Park Zoo in East Lansing. I loved those visits to the zoo and often wandered alone watching each exhibit especially the monkeys for as long as time allowed. I felt sorry for many animals in tiny cages — porcupines, raccoons, bears, opossums, etc. We never had soda at home but on this occasion, Ma gave us each ten cents to buy an orange drink.

Junior high was symbolically, high. Classes were now on the second floor with its panoramic views from the massive windows. I hadn't been on the second floor before starting seventh grade and had seldom been that high except for climbing the chute into the silo, but there were no vistas inside the chute. Speaking of chutes, one fire escape located in the library not far from the study hall was a huge tube, not unlike what one might find at a water park. To escape, one squatted down before an opened half-sized door, grabbed a horizontal bar above the doorway, and swung into the chute. It was always a special thrill on a fire drill day to be caught in the library or study hall rather than to have to use the old metal stairway fire escapes.

Three junior high teachers stand out. Miss Eastman, the math teacher in her fifties, is memorable simply for her stern looks and no-nonsense attitude. She did little to build my waning enthusiasm for the subject. We sat in rigid desks in rows with narrow aisles between, seats for about forty students.

Then there was Mrs. Stauffer, who was a veteran English teacher. In elementary school, I don't recall studying grammar. Mostly English was reading, penmanship, spelling, and vocabulary. Mrs. Stauffer attempted to teach us grammar and diagramming. At one point, she called me to her desk and tried to convince me that a sentence I had written, "We ain't got no eggs," was grammatically flawed. I simply didn't believe her. Everybody I knew in our farm community talked that way. After a couple D's on papers and continued attention to our grammar book, I began to think maybe she had a point, so I started to conform to her view, and my grades improved. I became so confident that I dared to start correcting others at home. That didn't go so well. Thus, I learned English as a second language.

Mrs. Shufelt, or as Pa referred to her — Mrs. Felt Shoe, was one of my favorites. She too was an experienced teacher of social science, geography, and history. She encouraged memorizing as a way of learning, and so I memorized all eighty-three counties in Michigan, the Gettysburg Address, *Oh, Captain, My Captain,* the Preamble to the Constitution, and much more. I think I already had learned the forty-eight states and their capitols. Yes, only forty-eight states until my senior year, and the pledge to the flag did not include the phrase "under God".

I missed most of seventh grade at Perry because I was bedridden with rheumatic fever. Instead, I had a county teacher for the homebound who came to the house twice a week. That experience is covered later. I had most of these same teachers in eighth grade, but I couldn't participate in physical education classes as I was still recovering.

Since our farm was at the far edge of the school district boundaries, ours was the longest ride to and from school — about seven miles if it had been directly to Perry, but much longer by way of many gravel roads, sometimes a mile or two off the main route just to pick up one child. If children weren't in the yard waiting when the bus arrived, the driver — for us that was Jim Hasford for most of my schooling — would honk the horn once or twice and if there was no signal from the house to wait a moment, off he'd go. I guess I remember Ma driving us to school once or twice when morning chores had complications that delayed us. While waiting for the bus, we often played made-up games in the front yard; Dave sometimes "tap danced" on the front porch to the latest pop hit, especially "Rockin' Robin", or we argued with the Kozumpliks who lived across the road.

On the nearly-hour-long bus rides to and from school, Henrietta, who became our class valedictorian, and I often studied together, drilling each other on facts for tests or details from reading assignments. Those bus trips had other distractions as well. In winter and spring, it wasn't uncommon for the bus to get stuck in a snow drift or mud so that we were sometimes an hour late getting to classes. Teachers couldn't mark us late or absent on those occasions and had to allow us to make up tests we may have missed. There were also fights now and then. Jim, our bus driver, was either unusually patient or chose not to stop for every little disturbance or pretended not to know what was going on in the back of the bus. However, if the situation grew serious enough that he had to pull over, suddenly there was silence in the bus and one or several students would be kicked off whether we were on a deserted gravel road or the main highway. I wonder how many times my older brother had to walk home and be punished at home for being late for chores.

For me, high school was primarily classes without extra-curricular activities unless the activities were during school hours. Farm work had priority. I was elected as a class representative to the student council two years, class historian one year, the role of announcer for the junior class play (no rehearsals were required), secretary and president of the Future Farmers of America, and class salutatorian. I was active in the Future Farmers of America (FFA), not only as an officer, but on competitive teams in public speaking, parliamentary procedure, and poultry judging. We also had competition to test our tractor skills — backing a trailer and a four-wheeled wagon and lining up pulley belts to other equipment. When the new high school opened, the FFA boys spent a lot of time raking and seeding and landscaping the lawn.

Besides required classes, I took speech, French, Latin, chemistry, agriculture, driver training, and farm shop. Senior boys were required to take Home and Family Living, a course designed to teach home budgets, housekeeping, marriage plans, child rearing, but hardly anything close to sex education. I took typing for a few days and dropped it to take Latin. Due to budget cuts, some years there were no phys-ed classes. Several teachers taught both math and gym or English and history or French and government or American literature and Latin. Some teachers I had for all four years of high school.

A few of my junior high teachers were also my high school teachers. I remember Mr. Lambert's nic-otine-stained fingers and how easily we could get him off the topic of discussion by asking a question about World War II. He was a veteran. Mr. Dunn taught everything from gym to math to English to driver's training. He and Miss Eastman forever tried to call me Dave. Obviously, Dave left a lasting impression on his teachers. Mr. Mason taught world history on the stage in the gymnasium. His first name was James, the same as the well-known actor, and most of the girls found him even more handsome than the actor. Then there was Mr. Blodgett, who taught biology and agriculture. I believe he was fired after two years. He had little con-trol over his classes of farm boys and on more than one occasion engaged in physical fights with them. Once, the students even removed him from the classroom! Mrs. Osten made learning French fun though our method of instruction was primarily reading, writing, vocabulary, translation, and pronunciation — almost no listening and speaking. Mr. Randolph mentioned to the American Lit class once that he liked raw eggs, so I brought one to class and invited him to "show us". He was a little cautious not knowing how fresh the egg might be, but I assured him I had personally gathered it the day before. He trusted me enough to crack it on his teeth and swallow it in front of the class.

In my two last years of high school when Dave had his own car and if he felt like allowing us to ride with him, we did occasionally go to football and basketball games and school DJ (disc jockey) dances. I didn't date at all in high school. I was too shy to even think about dating and didn't have a car and certainly would never have thought to ask for the family car. I didn't attend the junior or senior proms.

Dave was a senior when I was a sophomore and Dick was a freshman. We saw each other in the hallway and in FFA meetings and of course on the school bus with our sisters. All Perry students were dismissed at the same time, so first-graders through seniors all rode the same school busses. At the new high school, Jude, the oldest of my two sisters, was a freshman when I was a senior. We knew many of our siblings' classmates since many of them had brothers and sisters in our classes.

High school included weekly chapel services in the gym. Pastors from the various protestant churches in Perry and the priest from Morrice took turns addressing us. Chapel services included prayers by the clergy and often a hymn or two sung by the school choir or the Case sisters. I thought of the three Case sisters as our own version of the Maquire sisters, a popular trio in the '50s. Sharon, the oldest, was in my senior class. I believe the other two were a junior and a freshman.

I recall two field trips. One was to what we referred to as the insane asylum in Pontiac, Michigan. Just why we visited there as part of our biology class, I'm not sure. What I most remember are horrifying images of men sitting on the floor and chained to walls. Their stares, gestures, and groans were truly frightening to a naïve farm kid. As part of our civics class, we visited the county court house and sat in court for part of a trial. Ironically, the Kingston Trio had at that time a popular tune called *Tom Dooley* about a man sentenced to death which included the lines:

> *Hang down your head Tom Dooley*
> *Hang down your head and cry*
> *Hang down your head Tom Dooley*
> *Tomorrow you're going to die*

All high school students were bussed to Walled Lake Amusement Park outside Detroit for the end-of-the-year picnic. Of course, the roller coaster was a favorite, but I enjoyed every ride.

My senior class was the first class to attend the new high school, two years after the Mackinac Bridge was finished and the year before John Kennedy was elected. I understand that our class roster was placed in the cornerstone during construction. Ours was also the first, and probably the last, senior class to go on strike. One of our classmates, an excellent student, became pregnant and left school in her junior year. She continued her study through adult evening classes, completed all required credits, and asked to be allowed to graduate with her class. The school board denied her request. The matter was brought up as a part of business in a meeting of the senior class. Although the class was divided on the issue — mostly as a matter of the girl's morals — the majority supported her appeal and decided to confront the school administration. The administration felt obligated to obey the school board's decision. Much discussion continued among class members, especially in my speech class where we had been practicing debate techniques. Our teacher, finding a teachable moment, encouraged us to develop our argument and approach the board. We did so, but the board refused to hear us; thus, we chose to strike. We invited reporters from a local Lansing television station, WOAP (the Owosso radio station) and the *Owosso Argus Press*. I'm not sure they all showed up, but the television station did. Those of us supporting this girl simply walked out of our classes before noon and picketed in front of the school for perhaps an hour. I had never in any way broken any school rules, so this was scary behavior. Would I be expelled or punished in other ways? The television station aired our strike, and although I don't know how it happened — perhaps there was public response to the board's decision — but in the end the student was allowed to graduate with us along with, what I learned later, three other pregnant classmates.

Early in my senior year, the principal, Charles Randolph, who had also been my ninth-grade math teacher, Latin teacher, and my American literature teacher, suggested that I should take the SAT exam. I had never heard of it, but because of his strong positive influence on me, I checked with my parents to see if it was all right. Attending college was never a thought in my future. I assumed I would have a small farm and work in the Oldsmobile plant in Lansing and have a good life. However, I took the SAT at Michigan State University later in my senior year and despite the fact that some areas of the test were pure guesses, I did well enough to earn a full-tuition scholarship to Michigan

State. Now what to do? Pa couldn't see much sense in more schooling, but I think Ma convinced him to let me try, arguing that the farm wasn't big enough to divide between three sons. Thus, I had a green light to enroll, but since I was a first-generation college student, neither my parents nor I knew quite how to proceed, and we had no effective counseling at school. After reading and rereading the college catalogue, we understood that freshmen had to live on campus even though I lived only twenty miles from the university. That meant room and board expenses in addition to textbooks. I had saved a reasonable amount of money from raising pigs, so my parents wouldn't have to cover costs, at least not to start.

Another dilemma was what to study. As a farm boy, I knew that veterinarians had to go to college — and teachers and lawyers. Beyond that, I had no counseling about career choices. Furthermore, the number of majors was considerably fewer than those offered to today's students. I did well in math and science but was not passionate about either subject. I did, however, enjoy my English and literature classes and social sciences; thus, the choice was simple; I'd teach English and literature. What an accidentally fortunate decision that led to a wonderful 46-year career. I think Pa, who had an eighth-grade education, was a little embarrassed to tell farmer friends that I was going to college to be a "school teacher." In his mind, teachers were women. Even more confusing for him was to acknowledge that I was going to become an English teacher, of all things.

All the classes had fund-raising activities to save for the senior trip. We operated a candy store during lunch time and at sports events, had car washes, dances, donkey basketball games, and class plays among other activities. My 1959 graduating class went to New York City by train from Detroit through Canada. Most of the time we were closely chaperoned on tours of the Statue of Liberty, the United Nations Building, Rockefeller Center, the Empire State Building, and Ellis Island. We were allowed some freedom to explore on our own as long as we reported back on time, so some of my FFA friends and I took a subway to Coney Island. I was completely lost and hoping the other guys could get us back to the hotel. They did.

In the yearbook, I was voted by classmates as the quietest, the most serious, and the smartest; certainly not the best looking, most popular, most athletic, most girl crazy, or person everyone would like to know. As salutatorian of my class, I was seated on the stage during graduation and offered a brief speech restricted much by conventions. It was supposed to inspire classmates as they commenced into the adult world. I used all the techniques I had learned in speech class and delivered it with all the verbose wordiness and pomposity common for the occasion. I think both Ma and Pa were somewhat silently proud of me that day.

What to make of these years in the provincial Perry school system? I learned to memorize well. I didn't learn to think well. I had lots of acquaintances. I didn't have friends. I learned that obedience to rules was rewarded. Except for grammar in seventh grade, I didn't learn to question what I was taught. I discovered a little positive self-esteem from good grades. I didn't gain any athletic skills. I succeeded academically, but was woefully unprepared for college work.

4

Recalling High School 25 Years Later

I was invited to speak in May 1984 at the Perry High School Alumni Banquet to welcome the new class of graduates and to recall what it was like as a graduate twenty-five years earlier. Here is what I had to say.

Members of the classes of '84 and '59, alumni, ladies, and gentlemen. The class of 1984! When I was a senior, I studied George Orwell's novel 1984. Then, 1984 seemed like the distant future as I'm sure to '84 graduates, 1959 must seem like near antiquity. How much difference do twenty-five years really make?

I wonder, for example, if being a senior at Perry High School has really changed much since 1959.

I wonder if seniors still:
squeal tires in the parking lot, kiss by lockers, and go on senior trips
Do they still:
wear red and gray, cheer for the Ramblers, and sing the school fight song to the tune of "On Wisconsin"?

Do they:
sign yearbooks and smoke in johns?
Do they still compete:
with Corunna, Durand, and Laingsburg?
In '59, we used to:
exchange class rings to announce we were going
steady, get nervous about the future, and act cool.
Does all that still happen?
Are there still:
proms, senior plays, class meetings, and a course
called Home and Family Living?
Do they still:
imitate their rock idols and have disc jockeys
for school dances?
I wonder if they still:
tell moron jokes and go to drive-ins and
constantly switch radio stations
In '59, we used to:
spend hours looking at ourselves in mirrors,
lower our voices to swear, and fake our book
reports. Does that still happen?
We also used to:
get hassled by Mr. Potier. [the assistant principal]
Surely, that's not the same!
Do seniors still:
roll up their pant legs, pick homecoming queens,
and know more than their parents do?
Do they watch soap operas?
The Guiding Light and *Search for Tomorrow?*
Do they know:

Dick Clark, Vice President Nixon, Ann Landers, Al Kaline, and John Cameron Swayze?

Perhaps the more things change, the more they stay the same.

As a member of the first class to graduate from this building, one of my clearest memories is that of the night of the alumni banquet. That year, it was in the gym. The class of 1934 served as hosts. As I listened to various speakers that night, I tried to envision what life in 1934 must have been like. How was it similar to 1959? How was it different? How was it special? I'm still not sure I know.

My hunch is that today's graduates have a fairly clear conception of the late '50s having relived those years with *Happy Days* and *Grease* and reruns of *I Love Lucy* and *Leave It to Beaver*. They've heard of Howdy Doody and hula hoops, ducktails, and Edsels, bomb shelters, and blond bomb shells. Those things have nearly faded into history.

Nevertheless, we easily forget that what we have today wasn't always here. The recent film, *Iceman*, imagines the revival of a prehistoric man into our technological age. By some comparisons, I suppose we graduates of '59 are considered prehistoric. Had we hidden from progress and change, imagine our shock to arrive from 1959 to the world of 1984. What strange new machines would leave us confused? What terms would seem like a foreign language? How might we dress and eat differently? What dangers would we be unaware of? What might shock us? What history would have passed us by?

1959, for better or worse, as most of us know
it was a world without:
microwave ovens, instant coffee, light beer,
TV dinners, and electric toothbrushes.
We knew nothing of:
dishwashers, air conditioners, electric can
openers, and hair dryers.
We only dreamed of:
color TV, snowblowers, robots, cassette tape
recorders, and calculators.
We weren't protected by:
seat belts, the pill, security guards, and cigarette
warning labels.
We never heard of:
Xerox, condominiums, Women's Lib, and
computer dating.
We weren't entertained by:
video games, stereos, cable TV or FM radio.
We didn't wear:
panty hose, designer jeans, contact lens,
and mini skirts
Ours was a world without:
ten-speed bikes, Mustangs, computers,
digital clocks, and 2-liter bottles
We didn't fear:
PBB, herpes, AIDS, acid rain, and toxic
shock syndrome
How did we get by without:
shopping malls, instant replay, credit cards,
and McDonalds?

We weren't concerned about:
the energy shortage, the ozone level, drugs
and pot, the cost of gasoline, and PG, R, and
X ratings.
Names like:
Watergate, Muhammed Ali, Jimmy Carter,
and The Beatles *meant nothing.*

Well — What a bleak world those "happy days"
were! Lest we begin to confirm the suspicion that 1959
was indeed prehistoric, we need to be reminded that
for us graduates that year, the late '50s were full of
promise, progress, and change. Lots was new!

We brought with us into the '60s:
rock and roll, freeways, jet planes, and satellites.
We saw the invention of:
automatic transmissions, television, high-fidelity
records, and home freezers.
We witnessed:
the completion of the Mackinac Bridge,
statehood for Alaska and Hawaii, and
prevention of polio.
We put:
men into bermuda shorts, women into bikinis,
and teenagers into jeans
We liked:
Ike and Elvis
We first:
ate pizza, listened to transistor radios,
and fried in electric pans
We were first to read:
Mad, Sports Illustrated, and *Playboy*

And we were the first to graduate from the new Perry High School! True, it was only half its present size with a graduating class of fifty, but it was new, and we were first!

Well — twenty-five years do make a difference. And I think it would be terribly exciting to be starting again at commencement. I wish you all in the class of 1984 great success, adventure, and happiness in your next twenty-five years. I intend to be back here in the year 2009. Perhaps then you can tell me what's happened in twenty-five years. I'm anxious to know!

»» 5 «««

Romantic Fever

It was 6:00 a.m. that January morning when I, at age fourteen, tried to get out of my folding canvas army cot to go to the barn for morning chores. My brothers shared a double bed in the same room. They were already dressed and leaving the room when I collapsed on the floor, nearly fainting and unable to stand up because of my very painful joints. I had had a cold and sore throat for some time, but that was never enough of an excuse to not do my chores or go to school. We had to be *really* sick for that!

Pa had already left the adjoining bedroom assuming that all three of us boys had headed for the barn, but when Ma left the bedroom, I called to her to help me get up and get dressed. She helped me to sit on the edge of the cot and put her hand on my forehead to check my temperature. There was no doubt in her mind that I had a very high fever. She put me back to bed and covered me, then went to the barn to tell Pa and my brothers that I couldn't do chores that morning. And as it turned out, I didn't do chores for over a year.

I think Ma nursed me for a couple days — lots of liquids, Vick's VapoRub, cool washrags on my forehead, probably some aspirin, but I wasn't improving. My fever and painful knees, shoulders, and elbows persisted. Reluctantly, Pa finally agreed that I should see Dr. McKnight in Owosso, the same family doctor who had delivered me years earlier and had treated me when I was about six years old and was accidentally scalded by a dipper of boiling water Pa had spilled down my back when we boys were racing through the kitchen and bumped into him as he was carrying the water from the reservoir on the wood-burning kitchen range to the kitchen sink. Our family didn't have health insurance, so doctor visits were for broken bones, appendicitis, and baby deliveries.

After a fairly thorough check-up in his office, Dr. McKnight announced that I had rheumatic fever and that I must have absolute bed rest for a matter of months until the infection could be controlled. My rheumatic fever was the result of my untreated strep throat infection caused by streptococcus bacteria. Rheumatic fever can cause permanent damage to the heart since it causes infection and inflammation of the tissue around the heart. Ironically, it was my good fate to be struck with this infection in the early 1950s just after penicillin was becoming a common treatment for bacterial infections. Had I developed the disease a generation earlier, the outcome may have been considerably grimmer.

And so I began about six months of complete bed rest — bed pan and all. Fortunately, I wasn't hospitalized. I did not even once step out of bed during that time. When I went for doctor visits, Pa carried me to and from the car and into and out of the doctor's office. What a strange and wonderful experience to be lifted by Pa, who never hugged or held us even as small children. He allowed me to put my arm around his neck. I wasn't heavy, maybe less than 100 pounds at that time. I remained short and skinny through high school, probably stunted growth because of rheumatic fever.

I was transferred to the double bed and shared it with Dave. Dick moved to the cot. All my meals were brought to me, but I ate alone while the rest of the family ate together at the dining table. For a long time, I didn't have much of an appetite. I was prescribed vitamins and liver-tasting iron pills and antibiotics. Liver is one of the few foods I never could swallow — literally! For fiber, the doctor suggested I eat an orange a day. Oranges — an extravagance? — had almost never appeared in our house, so when Ma brought them home, it was clear to my brothers and sisters that they were only for me. As if I didn't feel guilty enough by having all my chores dumped on my brothers, these oranges also tasted like guilt to me.

The small first-floor bedroom was square and had two windows, one facing Brewer Road and the Kozumplik's house to the south and the other facing Ruess Road to the west. The bed was located so that I had a good view out both windows. The only additional furniture was an old three-drawer dresser — one drawer for each boy's stuff. I didn't have a radio, a clock, or a television, but the living room was just around the corner, so I could hear television and imagine. Most nights, the entire family stayed in the living room in front of the TV. Occasionally, they'd check to see if I needed anything — a drink, the bed pan, an extra blanket.

For the first few weeks, my brothers picked up homework from my teachers and returned my assignments. I really liked school and missed being in class, so this method of learning was miserable. After about a month, when it was clear that I wouldn't be returning to school for most of the school year, I was assigned to a teacher whose job was to teach homebound students throughout the county. Miss Marie Sleno was in her 30s, quite attractive, kind, and encouraging. I remember especially her perfume, something my mother very seldom wore. Miss Sleno came to the house two afternoons a week and spent two hours with me instructing and going over homework. She had about a dozen other students, and although I never met them, we exchanged homemade get-well cards and valentines.

When my parents had company, the guests usually visited me long enough to say hello. We farm kids seldom had friends who could visit. They all lived too far away. My sisters may have had a friend stay overnight, but seldom. My only regular visitors were Reverend and Mrs. Merrill, from the Bennington Methodist Church two miles away. They were probably in their sixties, but Mrs. Merrill was especially active with the Methodist Youth Fellowship. She brought me cards from other farm kids who attended there and books with Bible stories for young people.

In my first weeks away from school, my classmates, urged by Mrs. Shufelt, the social studies teacher, sent cards and get-well messages. In Perry Consolidated Schools, my class was perhaps fifty students, most of whom were my classmates since kindergarten, though by seventh grade, new students were added, being bussed from the rural districts which still had one-room first-grade to sixth-grade schools. One of my classmates was Pauline Kozumplik, who lived just across the road. One mid-March day about an hour after the school bus had brought my siblings home and my brothers were already in the barn starting their chores, I noticed to my horror out the south window a dozen wild girls crossing the road and running into our yard. Pauline was having an overnight birthday pajama party, so the girls decided to surprise me with a visit. I was shy by nature and had been isolated for months. Because of my disease, I was not supposed to be active or even emotionally stimulated to fun, anger, or excitement. I must have still looked like a pale, sickly mess. I was not ready for a dozen crazy girls to invade my small space. But that's what happened. They giggled their time away for about fifteen minutes while I crouched as far as I could under the blankets. Thankfully, Ma politely sent them on their way before I might have had a relapse.

I grew incredibly dependent on Ma, not just for my physical care — meals, wash cloth baths, haircuts, bed pan duty — but for my emotional wellbeing. My brothers and sisters spent little time with me. Mostly they were in school or doing chores and homework or watching TV with the rest of the family. Although I'm sure Pa worried about me, he very rarely came into the bedroom or even spent time at the door to ask how I was. Ma made time to read with me and help with homework. She'd put jigsaw puzzles on a piece of plywood on the bed so that we could work on them intermittently. As she went about her household chores — laundry, meals, dishes, house cleaning, driving to town for groceries, tending the basement wood-burning furnace, gathering eggs — she always made a point of telling me where she was and how long she'd be at it. When she returned from the hen house on cold, sunny winter afternoons, I could smell the fresh outdoors on her clothes.

Consequently, when my parents decided to travel to Florida in mid-February for ten days to stay with friends, I was emotionally devastated by the abandonment. My adult cousin, Robert Demerly, and his wife Harriet came to take care of the five of us and to help supervise the farm chores. From a parental viewpoint, I'm sure my parents thought they had everything covered. Robert and his wife, probably in their mid-20s, still "children" themselves, signed up for a responsibility way beyond their ability.

The second day after our parents left, I grew horribly homesick for Ma. I started crying around noon and continued even after the other kids returned from school. Seemingly, nothing they or Harriet could do could cheer me. By supper time, I began to sweat and feel weak, and then passed out for a short time. Harriet put cool wet washcloths on my forehead and decided she had better call the doctor. Back in 1954 in Owosso, at least one doctor still made house calls. Dr. McKnight arrived within an hour. I'm not sure that he did much because there probably wasn't much he could do. By the next day, I got over that intense loneliness.

In part, I think Robert and Harriet felt they needed to "play" with us. You can imagine how that sense of freedom from Pa's strict parenting and Ma's practical, common sense approach went over. Suddenly, my siblings were liberated! Dave had gotten a BB gun for Christmas that year and was ready to test it. Our "babysitters" drank Coke and let us try it. We had had pop only when it was served at the very few public events we might have attended. So charged with pop and a gun, you can imagine... From my vantage point in that small corner of the house, I recall one race through the bedroom, Dave opening the window in February and escaping out it pursued by Harriet laughing and yelling, "You can't get away that easy!" Another incident I learned about only after our parents returned is that Dave took a challenge to test the distance and accuracy of his BB gun. The target was the Kozumplik's huge new picture window way across the road. Dave was quite sure that his gun couldn't possibly shoot that far. He was proven wrong. The gun disappeared for a long time after our parents returned home.

Harriet did spend a lot of time in the bedroom with me and encouraged the other kids to as well. On one occasion, she set up our Uncle Wiggly board game — one from Ma's childhood — on the bed and got all my siblings to join us, all piled on the bed. Harriet weighed about 200 pounds. She was lounged on one corner of the foot of the bed on my side of the bed. Without warning sounds, that corner of the bed suddenly collapsed. The wooden leg had broken. We all slid toward her, as did our game. After the initial surprise, we had a terrific laugh. My brothers found an old cement block to prop up the bed. I think it remained that way until I recovered.

Before Ma and Pa left for Florida, they had asked each of us if there was anything they could bring us, like bananas and grapefruit. My answer was the same as it always was — a dog, specifically, a German shepherd like Rin Tin Tin. Pa had never been interested in having a farm dog believing dogs were a nuisance on a farm. They'd be running after the cattle and chickens, chasing cars in the road, barking at night, etc. He couldn't see getting a dog just to keep it chained up, so I knew it was rather futile, but I kept asking. In fact, to appease me, Ma had gotten me a dime-store ceramic dog, a small container for a house plant, the previous Christmas. It was a sad looking beagle puppy, cute, but no Rin Tin Tin.

When Ma and Pa returned after about ten days, they came with boxes of oranges, grapefruit, and tangerines and a huge bundle of green bananas — and a clumsy, lovable, very wiggly eight-week-old German shepherd puppy! Dave carried him into the bedroom and put him on the bed. So much for containing my emotional stimulation. This was beyond reality!

Unfortunately, I couldn't really play with him, but Ma or Dave or Dick brought him into the bedroom daily for short visits. He was to be a barn dog, not a house dog. He was certainly an incentive to get well as fast as I could. I wonder how it was that Pa ever consented to bringing me a dog. I think Ma might have applied a little persuasion. I learned later that Uncle Walt in Jackson knew of some puppies for sale when my parents stopped to see Aunt Vivian's family on their way home, so perhaps it was more than just Ma's persuasion. I want to think, and I do think, that Pa loved all his children even though he wasn't always confident in demonstrating his love, and this puppy was just exactly that, a demonstration of his love and compassion for me during that long winter.

I got letters. Aunt Veda and Uncle Lynn sent periodic cards from Detroit, often with small games and puzzles, as did Aunt Vivian. Most intriguing to me were letters from my mother's aunt Clara in St. Cloud, Florida. I think she was in her seventies or eighties at the time, but her penmanship was impeccable. I had never met her but had heard my mother's stories about her and her son, John Hamilton. Ma and her brother Lynn were the same age as their cousin and spent fun years on the family farm in New York as children until Grandpa and Grandma Wilson returned to Owosso. I sent thank-you letters in return and began correspondence with Aunt Clara until her death. I did meet her when our family drove to Florida for our Christmas vacation when I was in tenth grade. I remember her small frame house with lemon trees in the yard. She often wrote about her faith and after her death, I inherited her huge family bible with birth, baptism, wedding, and death records handwritten in it.

During that long convalescence, I became a voracious reader. I read almost everything that was available. That included Ma's old set of Nancy Drew mysteries, a couple books of children's Bible stories sent by Aunt Veda, the 18-volumn set of the Book of Knowledge that Ma had bought from a traveling salesman, library books my brothers brought home — especially biography: Daniel Boone, George Armstrong Custer, Thomas Jefferson, Davey Crockett, Teddy Roosevelt, Abraham Lincoln.... Miss Sleno brought me novels: *The Three Musketeers, Anne of Green Gables, Lassie Come Home, Call of the Wild...* I loved Ralph Moody's autobiographical *Little Britches* series, books with farm settings that I could identify with. I also read magazines. Francis and Alberta Halsey, for whom my dad had worked as a hired man and whom we kids thought of as almost grandparents, brought old magazines whenever they visited — *Saturday Evening Post, Life, Reader's Digest, The Farm Journal, Ladies Home Journal...* We had daily delivery of *The Owosso Argus Press,* and Pa always picked up a copy of the Sunday *Detroit Free Press.* We kids also had quite a supply of comic books that was constantly replenished through trades with our cousins in Jackson and the Rundells, neighbors a quarter mile away. I don't remember ever buying our own comic books, just recycling ones we'd been given. I liked them all — Superman, Dick Tracy, Donald Duck, Little Lulu, Blondie, Beetle Bailey, Marmaduke, Plastic Man, L'il Abner, Roy Rodgers... I think of this period of isolation as the catalyst for my later interest in literature and my eventual choice to major in English. Ironically, it was a privilege my brothers didn't have and may not have wanted anyway.

By mid-May, I was allowed to begin walking again. At first, that meant walking about fifteen feet to the bathroom and back. However, to my surprise, I couldn't. I expected to hop out of bed and head for the bathroom. Instead, my legs had weakened to such a point that they wouldn't allow me to stand on my own. I shook at the effort and grew faint; thus, my first several tries over a period of days were simply to stand by the bed for a short time. Then, by the end of the week with Ma's help, I could make it to the bathroom and back. Shall I say I was relieved? I was on my long way to recovery. I could now watch television and eat with the family again, but it was several weeks before I could go outside. In early June, when my brothers and sisters were still in school, I began to take short walks outside — to the barn to sit on a bale of straw with Spike, my German shepherd, to the chicken coop to sit on the steps and watch and listen to contented chicks scratching for food in their free-range territory, to sit on the front porch to wait for the return of the school bus. It was slow and easy for a long time — no chores, no "horsing around," no lifting.

It was a relatively lazy, luxurious summer for me though by summer's end I had begun to do most of my regular light chores, but I wasn't hefting bales, pitching silage, or shoveling shit yet. I returned to school but could not take gym classes. Instead, I was placed in an art class with thirty girls and one other guy. Girls didn't take gym classes. I learned to paint on glass, carve the top of a simple wood jewelry box, and crochet a cardboard/wallpapered sewing basket—all practical skills for life.

My recovery was complete. Years later, I easily passed my physical exam for military service except that my eyesight was too poor without glasses to qualify for a combat branch of the army; thus, I became an officer in the Medical Service Corps where I met optometrists who testified that my eyesight was good enough for me to take both airborne and ranger training. My heart condition wasn't a factor. Even in my seventies, I'm still running in 10K races.

Soon after I met Martha, we learned that we had both had rheumatic fever as teenagers. We like to think of it as having been in bed together for a year. Granted, she was in Wisconsin and I in Michigan. We had "romantic fever."

6

Being Schooled, Part II

Early in the summer of 1959, I visited Michigan State University for freshman orientation. I think it was a weekend with a night in a dorm. Rather than going away from this experience encouraged and informed, I felt more bewildered than ever. It wasn't just a matter of adjusting to dorm life and finding classrooms on this huge campus and learning routines; the methods of registering for classes and meeting my counselor and applying my scholarship and buying books were all baffling, and I had no personal friends or relatives to clue me in. I spent much of the rest of the summer worrying about this challenge and just what I was heading into. I recall nightmares of being lost on campus and failing tests.

In the third week of September, I left my last bunch of pigs to Dick, Jude, and Sal's care to be fed and marketed. Ma drove me to the campus about twenty miles away with what seemed like an antique suitcase we'd found in the attic and a cheap briefcase from Sears. On moving-in day, parents were allowed to come into the all-boys dorm, so together we met with the dorm counselor in the lobby, got my room assignment, and climbed to the third floor of Bailey

Hall and found my room halfway down the hall not far from the communal showers/bathroom. One of my two roommates, John, a sophomore from the Redford area of Detroit, was already settled in and had claimed the single bed leaving bunk beds for me and Steve, a freshman from Benton Harbor who arrived several hours later. I took the lower bunk, the second drawer in the one dresser, and a small portion of the closet — about the same way I had shared a bedroom with two brothers for years. I stuck my suitcase with extra clothes under the bed and wondered what to do with my briefcase and its contents since there was only one small desk in the room. It went under the bed, too, for the time being. Towels, pillows, and bedding were supplied. Ma didn't stay long. I walked her out and back to the car and told her I'd see her in a couple weeks knowing that I was expected home on weekends in the fall to help with silo filling, third- cutting hay harvest, and corn picking.

That first day or two was particularly awkward. I didn't know how to talk to strangers beyond perfunctory greetings. I answered questions my roommates asked as briefly as I could but didn't know how to ask them similar questions. They were both city boys whose life experience was very foreign to me. Steve and John were loquacious and easily bantered which was a relief, for I could just listen and keep my mouth shut. After settling in, they both went out to explore, and for John to greet old friends from the previous year. They probably invited me to join them. If so, I'm sure I declined with an excuse that I had to finish unpacking.

Communal showers, toilets, and bathroom sinks left me nervous. Remember, I had never had gym classes in high school. I tried to wait to times that I guessed the bathrooms would be empty. I brought pajamas, but since I had never worn pajamas at home, I wasn't even sure how to wear them. Were they to be worn over underwear? Should the shirt be tucked into the pants? Should I wear a t-shirt under the pajama shirt? I would just have to stall to see how the other guys did it.

Eating in the dining hall was another experience I had to learn. I had rarely eaten in restaurants, so again, I "followed the leader" to learn what to do. At times, I wasn't sure what the food was or how to eat it, so I avoided certain items or gradually tried small portions. Asparagus was one of those items. Before he married, Pa had worked as a hired man on a small farm that harvested asparagus, and as I learned the story over time, he grew sick of seeing asparagus when it was in season. The farm wife served it three times a day, and after weeks of harvesting, he'd had more than enough. Ma told us that after they got married, he said he never wanted to see asparagus on the table again but that he'd like potatoes three times a day. They compromised. There would be no asparagus, if the potatoes could be limited to twice a day. Thus, I grew up knowing that asparagus must be inedible. I knew from personal experience that liver was! Anyway, when I first noticed asparagus at the dining hall, I had to be told what it was. I deftly passed by it but noticed other guys seeming to really enjoy it and even going back for seconds. The next time it was served, I took one tiny spear. It wouldn't be too wasteful if I just took one bite. Wow! I had been deceived! What had I missed all my young life? It was delicious! Oh, the things one can learn in college!

That first term (Michigan State had not yet moved to a semester system), I enrolled in basic required classes — American Thought and Language (a humanities/composition course), natural science, and beginning French (two years of a foreign language were required for English majors). At that time, all male students were required to take two years of military science — either air force or army ROTC. I enrolled in army ROTC. Likewise, all students were required to take two years of physical education. That too was a totally new experience for me. Students had to declare that they couldn't swim or be tested for their swimming skills. I knew I couldn't swim and was eager to learn how; thus, my first gym class was beginning swimming in the nude in Jenison Field House pool. The humanities course was offered in temporary military Quonset huts which had been built to meet the needs of high post-World War II enrollment. French classes were in the very old Morell Hall, probably built in the 1880s. My counselor's office and most English and French classes were held there as well.

Once classes started, I began to develop a routine that depended on which classes met on which days and which times of day. Because the Brody dorms were on the far edge of the campus, I had to learn to adjust my walking time to not be late for classes. In spring, that also meant finding an alternate route across the Red Cedar River since the bridge and baseball field near Jenison Field House were often flooded. As simplistic as it may sound, I, for the first time, learned how to use an umbrella and began to enjoy its security on rainy days. I often made three trips back and forth across campus daily — to morning classes, back to the dorm for lunch, to afternoon classes, a return for supper (or what I was learning to call "dinner"), a trip to the library or Union Building in the evening and back to the dorm at night. Trying to study in the dorm was futile. With this routine, I was able to avoid socializing.

As that first term progressed, I continued to cope with shock. After receiving a D on my first humanities/composition paper, I learned how to make an appointment with an instructor. Getting a grade of D, and I was an English major? I learned how important it was at that time to use impressive vocabulary and fancy sentence and paragraph structure; that content seemed relatively insignificant. While sitting in this same class, I recall that during discussion, the name Michelangelo came up. Everyone in the room seemed to know exactly who this person was though I didn't recall seeing that name in the reading assignment. Naturally, I kept my mouth shut but soon opened my dictionary, as I very often did during my college years, to discover what everybody else had apparently learned in high school. In my swimming class, I learned how to use a combination lock and how to keep my towel wrapped around me until almost the second I slipped into the water and to have it handy as soon as I crawled out of the water. In ROTC, I learned how to polish brass and spit-shine shoes and stand at attention and salute. In first-year French, I learned how lucky I was to have had a year of French in high school. In natural science, I just barely learned how to keep my head above water (something I also learned in swimming).

Luckily, since in high school I had dropped typing to take Latin, I learned that many professors would accept some handwritten papers. When they wouldn't, I was most appreciative that Jude was willing to type them for me on weekends.

It wasn't until winter term that I began spending weekends on campus. In the fall, I arranged every Friday for a ride home with a farm neighbor who happened to work at the MSU pig barns. He drove me back to campus on Mondays. Again, it seemed to be a way to exclude myself from weekend partying on campus. I do recall one weekend when I stayed on campus that fall semester and got a free ticket to a football game. Freshmen were seated either in the end zone or in the highest seats in the stadium. During half time, the spectators were greeted by a team of Hollywood sound technicians who coached us how to make certain cheers that they hoped could be included in the film, *Spartacus*. So we Spartans produced wild jeers, enthusiastic cheers, and shocking gasps that were eventually included in the film. Imagine silent me in an Oscar-winning classic!

As that first term ended, it was apparent that some dorm room changes were imminent. John, the sophomore, had already arranged to move in with a friend he'd known for a year, and Steve was surely going to flunk out since he'd missed lots of classes and hadn't finished assignments. And so that winter semester of 1960, I was for a short time alone in the dorm and loving the isolation. However, within weeks, another guy named John was assigned to the room. He too was from the Detroit area, but at least he was more congenial than my first two roommates. The best thing about John was that he was madly in love with a hometown girl, so he had arranged his schedule in a way that allowed him to leave early on Fridays and return late on Mondays; thus, he was in the dorm only half the week. By spring term, he often skipped classes on Mondays and Fridays. I essentially had the room to myself. Had I scared them all away with my eccentric, silent existence?

In 1960, the voting eligibility age was 21; therefore, freshmen were not yet considered adults, so their report cards were sent directly to their parents. Grades would arrive just at or before Christmas. Though my grades weren't going to be all A's as I had become accustomed to in high school, I felt I had begun to get control of things by mid-term and would do well enough to retain my scholarship. Nevertheless, I worried, and when the report card arrived, my parents set it aside for me to open. I just couldn't open it right away. In fact, I let myself worry for a couple days before opening it. That became my pattern for the remainder of my four years at college. As it turned out, I received two C's (when C's were a very respectable grade), two B's, and an A (in swimming!) Believe me, I learned much more during that first term than is reflected in those grades.

During winter and spring terms, I spent most weekends on campus. My classes were a continuation of required courses but with new instructors. My physical education class was gymnastics, something I thought looked fun. On weekends, I did begin to break out of total isolation by attending a few basketball games, some gymnastics meets where one of my "assistant" instructors competed, a few dorm socials with guests from the women's dorms, one blind date for a tobogganing party, and church on Sunday mornings. For church, I walked about two miles to the closest Methodist church. Nobody went with me. I wrote to Dave in the Army in El Paso. By spring, I enjoyed walks along the Red Cedar to watch the ducks and ducklings and to study in the sun in some of MSU's beautifully landscaped gardens. There were also weekly military parades on the baseball field and the ROTC parade grounds with a drum corps and the colors and thousands of freshmen and sophomore cadets led by upperclassmen. In spring, noticing that most men were wearing bermuda shorts, I bought a pair. I had never worn shorts in my life. No farm or small-town boys I knew ever had. I wore them only on campus. It was daring enough to wear white buck shoes in high school, but to wear shorts at home would have been laughable.

After spending the summer on the farm, I looked forward to returning to classes in the fall of 1960 having retained my scholarship by improving my grades during the last two terms. Without pigs to support me, Pa allowed me to work part-time that summer. I had two jobs. First, I worked as a Christmas tree trimmer. No, I didn't put lights and ornaments on trees; I "trimmed" them; i.e., pruned them to the desired shape. I used hand pruning shears; I worked alone; I pruned about ten acres of trees in hot, humid conditions where any breeze was stifled by the trees. The most necessary pruning was above my head, so I was reaching up almost all day. Pa allowed me to bring his lunch-box-sized battery-operated transistor radio — my one escape from the tedium as I listened to Roy Orbison's *Only the Lonely* and Marty Robbins' *El*

Paso (thinking of Dave). The pruning season ended in July. I then worked as the hired hand for a neighbor farmer who had an industrial-sized corn sheller. In mid-summer, he began moving from farm to farm emptying the corn cribs which had stored government-subsidized storage of corn through the winter. My job was to help set up and take down the equipment and to do lots of shoveling inside the corn cribs of the corn on the cob to move it from the crib into a conveyor. I guess I earned about seventy cents an hour. Probably less.

One thing my parents and I learned from my first year of college was that I could have lived at home. In our naivete, we had read in the catalog that "freshmen must live on campus." The intended meaning was that they couldn't rent apartments. Of course, they could live at home with parents, but that isn't what we understood. Thus, now that Dick was also beginning classes at MSU, we both lived at home and commuted with two other local boys. We shared the driving and coordinated our schedules so that we'd arrive on time and not stay too late in the day. I didn't have a car, but Dick did, so he drove twice a week to take my turn at driving. Pa generously allowed us to use the farm supply of tractor and truck gas at about 30 cents a gallon, but the car probably got 15 miles to the gallon. We both continued to do full-time farm chores. I now think of that as the job that partly paid my way through three more years of college — no pay, but free room and board.

The farm house had an attic bedroom that Pa had built after the house was built. At the time, it was a room for Merton, one of his cousins who lived with us for a while. The only access was to go to the garage, up some stairs to the attic, and across the attic on loose boards to the small room. Dave had used this room before he went into the army. I think for him it was an easier way to come home late without being detected. Well, I claimed it as soon as I could as the most secluded place to study. There was one small window, one old double bed, a desk, chair, and lamp salvaged from the attic, and one feeble heat register. Though I almost needed a coat to cross the attic and garage in winter just to go downstairs to use the bathroom, I loved this privacy for study in the evenings and on weekend afternoons through the winter away from the television and other family commotion. It was my Upper Room.

The first televised presidential debates were that fall of 1960 — Vice President Nixon vs Senator Kennedy. It was an incredibly close race. Being an Owosso farm boy who was baptized Republican (after all, Thomas E. Dewey, twice a Republican presidential candidate, was born and raised in Owosso) and I, whose mother couldn't tolerate Harry Truman, naturally favored Nixon. In my expository writing class that term, we were asked to write an essay arguing reasons why we preferred one candidate over the other. I'm sure that essay simply repeated the major emphasis of Nixon's campaign — eight years of experience as Eisenhower's vice president and "tough on communism." I turned nineteen just after the election and the voting age was still twenty-one, so I was disenfranchised anyway. After Kennedy was elected, nearly the whole country, especially young people, agreed that the right man had won.

My sophomore year was filled with additional required courses including second-year French, ROTC, and physical education. This time I elected volleyball, badminton, and square dancing. The natural science class included geology and physics. My high school math and science only went so far as basic algebra and biology and chemistry, so the third term of this natural science class completely baffled me. It was only the luck of random guesses on an objective multiple-choice final exam that allowed me to pass. The sophomore year also required a more focused humanities class without the composition. We studied the art, religion, and literature of Egyptian, Greek, and Roman cultures, the Holy Roman Empire, the Renaissance, and 19th century art. This time through, I found out what everyone else already knew about Michelangelo. I also heard for the first time, the term "transubstantiation," the Catholic belief that bread and wine are truly changed into the body and blood of Jesus Christ. For a somewhat fundamentalist Methodist boy, this was stunningly incredible. For me, communion had been grape juice and little cubes of Wonder bread.

Pa had some difficulty understanding that Dick and I needed extra study time during final exams week. We could handle routine chores but asked that he postpone any additional projects until term break. By our teaming up and almost threatening to strike, Pa consented.

This second year seemed to pass quickly. In the summer of 1961, I pruned Christmas trees again and worked on construction for the same man who owned the Christmas tree farm. My construction work was primarily mixing cement, carrying bricks, and cleaning up. Part of that summer, I worked north of Owosso in a small factory that produced electric fencers and oven saver tins to be placed under pies as they're baked. My duties there varied. Some days I ran a simple press. Other days I packaged products for shipping, cleaned the shop, and unloaded supply trucks.

Returning to college as a junior in the fall of 1961, I was at last free to concentrate on my English major and history and French minors. I elected to continue for the next two years in the ROTC program to graduate with an army officer's commission. My thinking at the time was that there was no war, that I was very likely to be drafted as a private after completing college, and that the program offered a monthly stipend which would cover the cost of all of my textbooks and materials. I enjoyed this year delving into literature and linguistics, writing research papers, translating French literature, and sitting through history lectures. I had become a student at last! Reading novels and poetry, analyzing themes and characters and poetic techniques, and improving my writing skills were all pleasurable escape. My education classes, however, were seemingly irrelevant, philosophical, and dull. I was introduced to "transformational grammar", a new approach to understanding and teaching sentence structure. One memorable assignment asked us to pick a contemporary novel and to use several random pages for grammatical analysis of the author's sentence structure. I chose *To Kill a Mockingbird*, a novel I had purchased two years earlier through The Book of the Month Club I had joined. That novel's powerful theme particularly impressed me.

As an upperclassman in ROTC, I became a platoon leader for the spring parades. Jude and Sal agreed to be my recruits with whom I could practice drilling "raw troops." They didn't quite have a sense of military discipline and often fell into giggling spells, but still.... I joined the Pershing Rifles military honor society, and in my senior year was part of the honor guard carrying the colors during parades. During spring break in my junior year, I attended a brief "boot camp" at Fort Custer in Battle Creek. At that time, the camp looked very much like a World War II remnant with rundown barracks and poorly kept training areas. On campus, I was a member of the Pershing Rifles precision drill team. Occasionally, we practiced in the evening, so I had to catch a greyhound bus to Owosso. It left me off at Ruess Road, and I walked the mile home in the dark. I think there were twenty of us on the drill team who developed our own drill maneuvers using rifles with bayonets. We practiced and practiced again to the theme music from the movie *Bridge on the River Quai*. We tossed and twirled rifles and included a variety of fancy steps sideways, forward, and in reverse. Ultimately, we flew to New York City where we competed at Madison Square Garden. That was my first airplane ride — in a twin-engine forty-seater. Anyone who has ever marched or danced in a rehearsed unit with a memorized routine knows how a slight misstep by just one person can upset the whole routine. Well, that's precisely what happened at Madison Square Garden. After the misstep and bumbled confusion, we managed to regroup and complete the routine. A good lesson in humility.

In the summer of 1962, I spent six weeks at Fort Riley, Kansas, for officer candidate boot camp. In preparation for that, I started running up and down

Ruess Road and Brewer Road in my combat boots. It was an odd sight to see anyone running out in the country without a purpose such as an emergency at a neighbor's house or an effort to round up cattle that had broken out of the pasture fence. Until neighbors became accustomed to seeing me running, they would stop to offer rides.

I have several indelible memories of that summer in Kansas. It was incredibly hot! I had sunburned lips from hours on the firing ranges wearing a helmet that had no visor. I learned to love the Lister bag — a huge field water container made of canvas and propped on a tripod. The device was invented in a way that by a little breeze and evaporation, the water stayed relatively cool. A spigot or two at the bottom allowed us to fill our canteens. I met men from all over the Midwest and South. I also learned that I wasn't a very good marksman but that I could make my bunk so that a quarter would bounce off the blanket.

Already I'm a senior in the fall of 1962. The Cold War almost became a hot war that October when Soviet missiles were identified in Cuba. For a very tense week, everybody on campus crowded into lobbies and the Union Building — wherever there were televisions — to watch as Kennedy set up a naval blockade around Cuba and negotiated with Khrushchev to deescalate the situation. And here I was planning to join the army in a year. What relief when Khrushchev agreed to a supervised withdrawal of all the missiles!

My senior year was filled with literature classes — Realism and Naturalism in American Literature, Victorian Poets, The Age of Alexander Pope, Chaucer, Shakespeare, and English Literature in the Romantic

Period. And then there was Literary Criticism. I felt as lost in that class as I felt in the physics portion of that freshman natural science class. Nevertheless, I somehow put together a research paper offering a critical analysis of the religious themes in *Moby Dick*. Why did I pick almost the longest novel in American literature? I received an A on that project, but I'm convinced that the length of the essay encouraged my instructor to give it a superficial glance, and to avoid having to explain a lower grade, simply slapped on an A.

I've forgotten the names of almost all my instructors, but I remember a few of their eccentricities. There was the humanities instructor whose favorite phrase when referring to the promises politicians make was, "There'll be pie in the sky by and by." I recall only one female instructor in those years, a teacher of ancient history. She was very commanding in front of 200 students in a lecture hall. I much respected her. Another instructor used to pace the front of the room with a rubber band in his hands. He'd twist and untwist it around his fingers. I was so distracted wondering how blue his fingers would become before he would release them that I often paid little attention to what he had to say.

Throughout my life up to this point and through my college years, I was very solitary, bookish, quiet, and mostly non-social. I didn't have close friends. True, I had been a class officer in high school, involved in 4-H club activities, president of the Future Farmers of America chapter, active in the Pershing Rifles drill team, and committed to church youth activities, but those were perfunctory roles that didn't require closeness. I never dated. I didn't have a best friend. I certainly never bonded with my college roommates. When we were children, I felt close to my siblings and played and talked with them and had lots of fun even doing farm work together, but that gradually changed as my brothers became teenagers because after my years of recovery from rheumatic fever, they had farm responsibilities that I couldn't share. They became much more interested in cars and dating than I ever did. And, of course, I could never talk with Pa. My sisters were fun for teasing.

Ma was my one reliable confidant with whom I could almost always feel free. I'm sure everyone of her children felt just as I did. Although she "laid down the law" when necessary, she more commonly encouraged us and noticed our little successes — learning a Biblical passage for recital at church, getting a third-place 4-H ribbon at the county fair, winning the class spelling bee, and being polite and kind to others. I think she particularly enjoyed our teen years — our silly music, our clothing fads, our school gossip, our more adult-like help on the farm, our deepening religious faith. She had a special way of patching us up after accidents since without insurance, we rarely visited the doctor and never a dentist. There were Sal's and Jude's broken arm and leg, scalding hot water spilled down my back, Dick's foot chopped with an axe, lots of minor cuts and bruises, measles, mumps, the flu, and constant colds in the winter. For a little while, we'd have her full attention, but before long, we were expected to "get back in the saddle."

For me, our bond grew stronger during my year with rheumatic fever and thereafter as I slowly convalesced. During that time, I was almost completely dependent on her. Now during those last three years of college, she was often a willing sounding board as I talked through my analysis of a Theodore Dreiser novel or a Shakespearean comedy or the prewriting of a research paper on the Constitutional Convention. She'd be ironing or peeling potatoes or patching overalls as I tossed ideas out. Probably much of what I proposed was incomprehensible, but she'd periodically nod and smile or say, "That sounds good," or ask, "Is there really such a word as "incontrovertible"? Sometimes she'd just mutter, "If you say so." I think she enjoyed having me as a distraction from the tedium of her chores. Later she often asked how that paper on Charles Dickens went or how I did on my test on Victorian poets. We, or at least I, enjoyed these "study sessions."

Most of my college years were during the Kennedy presidency, that of the youngest president ever elected. His presidency and its optimism directed toward the post-war generation had a great influence on me. I was inspired by his proclamation that we ask not what our country can do for us, but what we could do for our country. I felt encouraged to continue toward military service, but even more, I was impressed by his creation of the Peace Corps. Since I was already committed to two years in the army after graduation, joining the Peace Corps wasn't an option at that time, but the possibility remained in my thoughts. These years were also the beginning of the Civil Rights Movement with Dr. Martin Luther King's leadership to influence and inspire me.

I didn't graduate in the spring of 1963 with most of the rest of my class because I needed to complete student teaching, a semester of course work that I couldn't fit in earlier. That summer I worked at Owosso Memorial Hospital where I was born. I was a yard maintenance man under the supervision of an older Czechoslovakian immigrant. I liked his style. He proposed that we work hard during the morning and early afternoon mowing lawns, weeding flower beds, pruning shrubbery, hosing sidewalks, picking up branches and litter and cigarette butts, emptying outdoor trash cans, etc., and then in the late hot afternoons still on the clock, we'd be "at work" somewhat less visible somewhere on the hospital property — usually behind a utility shed reading a novel.

I bought my first car that summer at age twenty-two, a necessity for traveling to Jackson, Michigan, where I would live with my aunt and uncle and cousins while I began to learn to teach at Jackson High School. Pa helped me by finding a neighbor's ugly green eight-year-old Plymouth, mine for the taking at eighty-six dollars, if I remember correctly. I named her Lemon-Lime. She was lime-colored and was most certainly a "lemon."

In August of 1963, I packed up and moved to Jackson for my last semester of college. My cousin Scott had just returned from serving in the army in Europe. His sister Jan was a senior at the high school, and Susan was in middle school. Aunt Vivian worked as a stenographer and office manager for the Jackson branch of the Michigan Department of Social Services, and Uncle Walt continued his decades of work as a guard at the Jackson Penitentiary. This family of Ma's sister were our closest relatives. These cousins had at various times spent summers with us on the farm, celebrated holidays with us, and once vacationed with us at Pentwater State Park, but they were "city kids" and had grown up in circumstances far different from my youth on the farm.

After a week of my settling into their lifestyle, all of us young people returned to school. Scott was taking classes at the community college, and most days, Jan rode to and from school with me in Lemon-Lime. As the weather grew cold, Lemon-Lime grew reluctant to start, and the defroster didn't work. On one particularly frosty morning when I was bent over the steering wheel peering intently through a post-card-sized clear spot on the windshield, the car stalled on railroad tracks. There was no impending train/car collision, and both Jan and I managed to push the car off the road and off the tracks. After several tries, Lemon-Lime stuttered to life — just another of her near-death experiences (and mine).

My supervising teacher, Dorothy Rich, was an excellent, very experienced, heavy, white-haired, English and journalism teacher nearing retirement. She allowed me to observe her classes for a couple weeks and gave me other classroom preparation, individual tutoring, and correcting responsibilities while I became familiar with texts and began to plan for the two classes she chose for me to teach — a tenth-grade English class and a junior American literature class. Mrs. Rich could very casually lead classes in an hour of fascinating discussion of a short story or a few poems. How did she do it? I began to learn that my college classes in educational psychology and methodology were far too abstract to be practical. I would learn by doing under the wonderful and patient direction of my master.

I spent hours in preparation for every class writing out dozens of questions to generate discussion, writing exams and correcting essays, finding imaginative ways to review for tests, creating instructional bulletin boards, and keeping students motivated and challenged. The American literature students were studying early and mid-nineteenth century writers like Thoreau, Emerson, Hawthorne, and Poe. At the same time, America was remembering the 100th anniversary of the battle at Gettysburg. As a history minor, I enjoyed making relevant the literature of that period to the war and daily life of rural and urban Americans of the mid-1800s.

During the last class of the day on Friday, November 22nd, one of my tenth-grade students asked to use the restroom. When she returned a short time later, she entered the room and almost nonchalantly announced that someone had shot the president. The students reacted in ways that said, "Come on. Stop making up stories." I asked her to sit down, but she persisted, saying she wasn't making it up. Just then an announcement came from the principal's office over the school's intercom system. The president had been shot in a motorcade in Dallas. Classes were dismissed early. Students were to leave the building. Busses would arrive soon. Nobody moved. It just didn't seem possible. How could it be that such a young, charismatic, popular president and father would be shot? There were very few further details, only that he was rushed to a hospital.

After the students left, I wandered the school halls for a while, perhaps in shock. I followed a few other teachers into the auditorium where radio broadcasts were carried over the speakers. Still there was no news about the seriousness of the injuries. I prayed for him and his family as most of America must have been at that moment. Soon after I arrived at my aunt and uncle's home, we learned that the president had been killed. Thanksgiving Day was the following Thursday. Classes were cancelled for the whole week. I had planned to go back to the farm for the holiday, but chose to stay in Jackson in front of the black and white television while I and the whole nation watched the sad drama unfold—the capture of Lee Harvey Oswald, the swearing in of the new president, the arrival of the president's plane in Washington D.C., the assassination of Oswald on live television, the long lines of mourners at the capitol building and along the funeral cortege route to Arlington Cemetery.

My classes continued for only two weeks after the assassination because Michigan State's semester ended. I had grown very fond of my students and would miss them. They were aware that I would soon be going into the army and had farewell parties for me on the last day. My sophomore class, perhaps with Mrs. Rich's help, had arranged to have a personalized leather wallet made as a parting gift. It had my initials and the American eagle carved into the leather — the work of a prisoner at the penitentiary. A couple of these students continued to write to me while I was in the army.

On a Friday afternoon on December 6th prior to graduation, the ROTC command held a commissioning ceremony for fall semester graduates. Ma and Sal attended and pinned on my 2nd lieutenant bars and my caduceus insignia indicating my assignment to the Army Medical Service Corps. I was not eligible for a combat branch because of my poor eyesight. I would report to Fort Sam Houston, Texas, in March for three months of specialized officer training prior to being sent to Fort Ord, California, for my permanent assignment.

That same evening, Michigan State held its fall graduation ceremonies in the auditorium, the same building where I had first registered for classes back in 1959 and where I had a near-front seat when Carl Sandburg lectured. I had passed the auditorium on foot daily from the parking lot to classrooms when commuting to the campus during my last three years at MSU. We had gone home after the earlier ROTC commissioning ceremony, and since I needed to be at the auditorium an hour before the graduation ceremonies were to begin, my parents and I drove separately. Sal rode along with me. How then was it possible that I got lost on campus trying to find the auditorium in the dark? Perhaps Pa was right when he occasionally said I had a lot of book learning but very little practical common sense. Several of the familiar routes had been blocked off to accommodate graduation traffic. Furthermore, I had very seldom driven on campus since I hadn't had a car. Well, eventually, it was Sal, who had been on campus only a few times for marching band events, who suggested we turn "here." I spotted my destination and although we had to park some distance away, we got there in time for the procession.

I received my bachelor's degree in English with minors in French and history and a Michigan secondary teaching certificate. Wow! All that on top of my army commission? With all the pomp of the university band and orchestra, the colors of the professors' robes, the procession of graduates, and the laudatory words of the various speakers, I was convinced that at last Pa with his eighth-grade education might have begun to think that perhaps all this schooling added up to something after all. After the ceremony, I met Ma and Pa in a gathering area where I introduced them to Mrs. Rich, who said she wouldn't have missed it. Her comment to my parents that she was confident I would be an excellent teacher left me very touched and confident of my somewhat accidental career choice.

⇛ 7 ⇚

Memories of Ma

The following two memory pieces are organized using prompts from a teaching colleague, Peter Putnam, who at the time was writing a memoir of his father. My responses extend beyond those "first years".

10 Questions

What smells do you associate with your mother?
Fudge cooking as we ran to the house after getting off the school bus.

When you picture your mother, what one or two details stand out for you?
Warm hugs, smiles, happy eyes, delightful chuckles.

What was your mother's favorite thing to eat? To drink?
She was a coffee drinker and seemed to like almost any food — especially if she didn't have to prepare it. She sat at our table at the position last to serve herself, so it wasn't uncommon that she got scraps, but she never complained. She didn't like beer and referred to it as "horse piss".

What was your mother's favorite word or phrase or saying or joke?
"Dry up and blow away" "Darn it anyway!"
"Hold your horses" "Don't bust your britches"
"Use it up, wear it out, make it do, or do without" "Don't put off till tomorrow what you should do today" She found nothing favorable to say about Harry Truman.

If your mother were an animal, what animal would he be?
A hen protecting her chicks.

What specific songs or music did your mother listen to, dance to, whistle, or sing while you were growing up?
Familiar old hymns, the Polka Hour on Owosso's WOAP Sunday radio, The Grand Ole Opry, Lawrence Welk, lots of country music, (and for her amusement) music of the '50s when we were teens.

If asked to put a hand on the part of your body where your mother wounded you, where would you place it?
It never happened.

If asked to put a hand on the part of your body where your mother blessed you or where you wish your mother would bless you, where would you place it?
My head, heart, and soul.

If you had to choose one item or object to symbolize your mother, what would you pick?
Letters from home when I was far away.

Three Lists

List #1: "Ten Things I Did to Win My Mother's Love."

Went to church

Didn't fight in the house

Tried to be polite

Worked hard at school

Teased her

Wrote home often when I lived at a distance

Helped in the house

Admired her three husbands

Stayed out of trouble

Tried to solve my own problems

List #2: "5 Things I Carry of my Mother's Shadow." By "shadow" here, I mean inherited or adopted traits or behaviors of your mother that you judge to be negative.

Passivity?

Love of desserts

List #3: "Five Things I Carry of my Mother's Gold." By "gold" here, I mean inherited or adopted traits or behaviors of your mother that you judge to be positive.

Open-mindedness

Empathy for others

Religious faith

Love of animals and nature

Love for travel and adventure

Love of family

Hard work

Letter writing

Frugality

Common sense

Two Prompts

Prompt #1: "Ma, I remember"

All your special care with just the two of us in the house while I recovered from rheumatic fever

Your allowing us kids to pick out a possible Christmas gift from the Penney's and Sears catalogs

Your fanning the bed sheets over us when you put fresh sheets on the bed at bedtime

Your reading your old school books to us at nap time on the floor of the front room in the old house

Your playing cards and board games and putting puzzles together with us

Your letting us choose the birthday cake we'd like (always chocolate for me)

Your patching worn-out old torn overalls and jeans

Your smooching with Pa in the car while listening to country music as we kids swam at Round Lake

Your standing behind Pa's chair and tickling him inside his bib overalls at the kitchen table

Your taking us trick-or-treating in Owosso
in the old farm truck

Your teaching us some fundamental cooking
— especially desserts

Watching you scald, gut, and clean chickens

Your amusement at our teenage fads, music,
fashion, and conversation

Seeing you reminisce with your brothers
and sister

Camping all over Michigan and in Florida
in our 16-foot camper trailer

Your hospitality to whomever showed up at
the door. This was often Uncle Orlin who
seemed to know just when our dinnertime
was or your high school friend who gratefully
ate our leftovers no matter what time of day.

Seeing you in the bleachers as I delivered
my salutatorian's address at my high school
graduation

Your taking me to the college dorm when
I first started college

Your tolerating my blabbing about
college course work

Your attending my army officer's commissioning ceremony and college graduation

Your picking me up at Fort Benning after
airborne training

Your letters to me while I was in the army,
Hawaii, Malaysia, and Australia

Your welcoming my "strange" adult friends
from the army and Peace Corps

You and Pa driving the farm truck with our belongings when Linda and I first moved to Detroit; Pa letting you out a block or two from the house so that you could read the house numbers as you walked and he followed in the truck.

Your profound loss and sadness at Pa's sudden death

Your cute embarrassment at falling in love with and marrying Francis and news of your engagement

Apple picking on the farm with almost all the grandkids

Your care for Francis in his last year with cancer

Your sorting through items after Francis' passing to be sure that we "kids" got any items that you could give away before the estate sale

My driving you home from Florida with a stop in Renfro Valley

Your courtship with Lawrence, sending him letters while you were visiting at the cottage

Visiting you in the hospital after your first heart attack

Saying goodbye at your modest funeral

Prompt #2: "Ma, I don't remember"

Your going to church with us

Your ever swearing beyond "Darn it anyway!"

Your saying anything positive about
Harry Truman

"Painting" the Best Memory/Worst Memory
of Your Mother

Ma, some of my worst memories were the
times I first caught you smoking when I was
about 15

You got mad at our puppy after I let her race
through the strawberry patch spilling boxes
of berries while you were picking them

You left me when I was sick to travel
to Florida

You attended the sixth-grade Mother's Day
party (Shame on me!)

We were planning Pa's funeral

I walked in while you were crying in the
afternoon three years after Pa's death

You had a heart attack

A Letter to your Mother

Hi Ma,

I like to think you and Pa are having a great time
together again, laughing and "smooching" and sitting
quietly in confident love for each other. You two were
quite a team building the farm and building a family,
each of you contributing what you could in the ways
that you could. I understand a little better now what I
couldn't have known then about all the hard work and
collaboration it must have taken, yet you found time for
camping and travel, picnics in the park in Owosso, card
games, Sunday drives to visit neighbors, relatives, and

friends, and trips to Florida, the west, and Canada.

It would be fascinating to know how you talked with Pa about us kids because you never talked in personal ways about the children when any of us were present. I'm sure you were sometimes exasperated; I'm quite sure you and Pa didn't always agree on the degree of rowdiness you allowed when he wasn't in the house; I wonder if Pa ever expressed pride in anything I did as a kid. I could see his pride in Dave and Dick as they mastered farming in ways I never did, and I know he delighted in Jude and Sal who could gently tease him in ways we boys would never think of doing. He must have worried considerably about doctor expenses when I had rheumatic fever and whether I'd ever become very useful. Did you laugh together at our various antics and stunts and mishaps? Did Pa pay much attention to our school activities?

You were always my constant encourager in your typically modest way, sometimes by just listening (and writing letters). You always let me know (as I'm sure you did with all of us) without even saying anything how proud you were of my smallest achievements — winning a sixth-grade spelling bee, giving a sermon at church on youth Sunday, being elected president of the FFA, being chosen as the senior of the week by the *Owosso Argus Press*, going with the ROTC precision drill team to Madison Square Garden, starting my student teaching while living with Aunt Vivian, heading to Australia with my new family, and so much more. And you were always there if you could be for my "major" achievements — salutatorian at my high school graduation, induction into the army as an officer in the Medical Service Corps, my college graduation with Michigan secondary education certification, my graduation from airborne training, and both of my marriages.

I was touched by your welcoming embrace of both my adopted children and my stepson, Mike, who you loved in the same way you loved all your grandchildren, and I much appreciated your non-critical support as I struggled through separation and divorce from Linda. Most of all, I rejoiced at your bonding with Martha and her with you. You would have been touched by the eulogy she offered at your funeral.

I have lots of treasured items around the house and cottage to remind me of you — some simple framed art, a few old toys you had as a child, several Christmas ornaments, boxes of old photos, letters you saved from me during my military, Peace Corps, and Australian years, your great grandpa's homemade pull-down desk, your dad's law bookcase, salt and pepper shakers you kept on the stove all the years we were young, a number of kitchen utensils which are as good as ever, a wicker-seat rocking chair, and several books from my childhood.

Perhaps you already know that my son, Dave, passed away at the age of 33 just a year after you did. It was such a sad ending for a boy who brought such delight. I hope that you and Pa and he and Jude have enjoyed eternal life together. His daughter, Brittany, is nearly thirty now. You would be as proud of her as I am. Despite her early childhood in near poverty without much education beyond fifth grade, she has "pulled herself up by her bootstraps" and has become a certified nursing assistant. Three years after you passed away, Angela and John had twin daughters who are now in high school. You would love them and their older sister, Kara, who you knew as a baby. Kara is now a university student in Cincinnati. My stepson, Mike, who remembers you very fondly, was married briefly and seems to be increasingly finding contentment in his life. That's all for right now. I love you, Ma. Thanks for the life you gave me. I look forward to a wonderful reunion with you in eternity.

Ed

A Letter from your Mother to you

Dear Ed,

Since last we were together, I've kept my eye on you and heard your conversations with me through prayer. I know you drifted away from faith for a number of years, but I'm so glad you found your way back and that you're so active in your church. It's just like you to be a leader on that Justice and Peace committee and to try to bring about understanding and respect between religions. I chuckled a number of times when I heard you defining heaven for your fifth-grade catechism classes, that it wasn't necessarily up in the clouds far away, that it was probably all around us but invisible to our senses, that in fact, you were quite sure that I was sitting over in the corner watching the lesson. I was!

I'm so happy to see how you and Martha are so generous in sharing your relaxing cottage with so many friends and relatives and especially with Mike and his friends and Angela"s family. And then to open your "boarding" house to Johannes and Loic and that doctor, Mike, and now Rachel and yes to Veda as well when she especially needed help. Thanks for helping Lynn in his final days and for continuing to look after Veda.

Martha was so gracious to speak at my funeral. Oh yes, I was there! I was very grateful that you offered to speak at both Jude's and Lynn's funerals. I also listened in as you gave eulogies for Martha's parents, but my heart was really saddened to hear you speak at your son's memorial.

I see you finally retired after a long lifetime of teaching. You were just meant for a job like that, and I'm sure lots of your former students remember you well. I watched as you got that language institute under way. You have a special way of communicating with foreign students.

Since I left you, you've been pretty busy over the years researching the Demerly roots. It's amazing what you've found out. Now how about the Wilson/ Ford roots? You can find some of that in the boxes of old photos I left. I was happy that you got to Scotland and looked around for a little Wilson history there.

You were president of the College English Association. I bet Martha nudged you into that. If so, good for her. As a kid, you were more likely to do the grunt work than take the lead.

It's good to see that you're still "farming" in your good-sized garden and flower beds. You always were the one most likely to wander into our garden when I was out there picking beans or weeding, and then you'd pitch in.

I'm in good company here with my brothers and sister; Pa, Francis, and Laurence; Kellie, Mike and Andy and your David; Diane and Bev, and much too soon, Jude. I've had some really good visits with Martha's parents as well.

Keep doing God's will on earth as best you know how to. I look forward to one of your generous hugs one of these days, but there's certainly no hurry. I'm keeping my eye on you.

Love,

Ma

A Letter from you to your Daughter

Hi Ang,

I haven't written you a letter in a long time. E-mails, texting, and phone calls seem to have taken over. But I think of you more often than you might imagine, so I thought I'd put a few of those thoughts in a letter.

I'm really glad that fate somehow brought us together from opposite sides of the world. I started loving you months before I met you at the Chicago airport where you were terrified of me in my bushy beard. The first photos we saw of you at age four in your little knit sweater squinting into the sunlight at the Korean orphanage told me, "She's the one who most needs a home, and we're the ones who most need a daughter."

That first year was a challenging one as you grew healthy after years of malnutrition, scabies, and tapeworm infestation. You had had very little loving social interaction and almost no education. You didn't know how to hold a crayon or pencil or book. There you were in a very strange culture, certainly terrified and pleading for your Korean escort at the airport to not leave you though you didn't seem able to cry. When she abruptly turned away and left, you held tightly to your new mom all the way on our flight to Detroit on that rainy April 22, 1975, day.

In the first weeks and months (and even years) with us, it was Dave who made all the difference. He so generously and gently shared his toys and time and had you beginning to speak a little English within days. He coaxed you to giggle and read books to you and allowed you to imitate almost everything he did. Still, your insecurities persisted for weeks. Though we had prepared a beautiful bedroom for you with some stuffed toys and dolls and brightly painted furniture, you preferred to sleep on the floor as you had done in Korea, and in the night, you often crept quietly into our bedroom and slept on the floor beside our bed. Once you understood where the kitchen was, you often went downstairs in the dark and sat alone at your place at our small table waiting for food to appear. One day you were so exhausted that while we were eating supper, you fell asleep and nearly fell off your chair. In Mom's attempt to catch you, she wrenched your shoulder, so you had several days of pain, but that too passed.

Although you had been in the US only four months, after consultation with the kindergarten teacher at Duvall Elementary, we all agreed that you certainly were not kindergarten ready but that joining a class would be very beneficial in learning English and social behavior in this still strange land. You flourished! In just a short time, you looked forward to class days. Even so, your teacher and we agreed at the end of the school year that it would be to your great advantage to repeat kindergarten so that you would enter first grade fully prepared. Halfway through that second year, you were so ready to move on! I think that extra year gave you the confidence to pursue your education with confidence all the way through your bachelor's degree.

I loved having you as a kid! You always wanted to help out. You wanted to know how everything worked. You wanted the world around you happy, and you worked to make it so. Remember your diligent swim lessons? Your piano recital which was really beautiful, but you wanted rock 'n' roll. Movies with Dave at Fairlane — especially *Grease*? Remember your part in *The Wizard of Oz*? Remember your record-breaking sales of Girl Scout cookies and your summers at Girl Scout camp with spiders in the tents? Remember our great western camping trip where you did much of the putting up and taking down of the tent? And trips to Washington and Florida and New England and around Lake Superior? Remember picking strawberries and apples and cleaning and freezing strawberries together and making apple pies? You loved helping in the kitchen, and I loved having your help.

I know how painful and frightening your mom's and my divorce was for you and Dave. I tried to ease that a little by finding a rental home nearby. You busily biked back and forth between our homes. I was glad to have your friends there with you after school and missed days that you weren't there. In that period of your mom's and my separation, I recall that we both attended a school concert where you had a part. As we were talking after the event, you came up and tried to get us to hold hands — typical of you.

And what a transition when you chose to live with Martha and me after my remarriage. Not only was it new friends, three new schools in one year, two new houses, and a new brother, it was adjustments to a new family life. You ambitiously took on your house-cleaning chores (for the love of allowance money?). Although Martha and I encouraged you to join clubs and sports at school, you insisted you wanted to work part time, and so you found work at a lawyer's office and later as a waitress at a number of restaurants over time where you hauled home tips twice as large as your pay check. You graduated with excellent grades and not knowing a soul there, headed off to Kalama-zoo College. It wasn't always easy, but you survived it and did well at Southfield Lathrup High. I'm proud of you, Angela.

I really had mixed feelings of pride and sadness the day we headed for Kalamazoo College. You were so ready for the challenge and independence. I knew that, but it all seemed to happen too suddenly. I'm proud of your determination to work hard at both your studies and various jobs during your college years to help cover a great part of your expenses. Then you were on your way to Japan for six months, teaching high school in Lansing, and finally graduation. Then before I knew it, you were moving to Cleveland, and why not? You found work and an apartment, and independence — a frightening possibility for many women at that time, but you managed it well. You've now lived there longer than you've lived anywhere.

I'm glad you chose John and together have raised three fine daughters. That doesn't just happen, does it? It takes constant attention every day of their lives, and you've done that so well — getting them into sports activities, guiding their academic lives, teaching them common courtesy and respect for others, offering an excellent example of work ethic, allowing them to have fun, and directing their faith lives. You have every right to be proud, Angela.

I love you,

Dad

Photo Album

My Demerly grandparents, Andrew and Josie, with their five surviving children – Garold, Clyde, Leora, Jake, and Shirley (my dad).

Enjoying a leek soup supper with the Tamerl family in Austria, 2006. Gilles Demmerle, second from left.

Family reunion in Etting, France, 2006. Gilles is in the center with Martha and me.

Ma and Pa in Benzonia, 1938.

Pa and Ma with Dave, my older brother, soon after moving into the granary home, 1939.

Dave on the back porch, 1940.

My siblings and me in the front room at Christmas with dolls and
six-shooters, about 1948. Left to right – Jude, Ed, Dave, Dick, and Sal.

Pa doing the milking, about 1948.

Pa at the sawmill, 1949.

Pa sharpening the saw, 1949.

The new house in the mid-1960s with the remodeled barn, new sheds, new silo, and camper trailer. The second building from the left is the old granary house remodeled as a farm workshop with an upstairs chicken coop and a built-on shed. The Kozumpliks' home in the foreground.

Remodeling the barn in the mid-'50s.

The old Perry high school with its 1922 addition. (copied from 125th Anniversary History of The Perry School District 1881-2002).

My fourth-grade photo with my first pair of glasses.

Feeding some of my pigs, 1957.

Giving Spike a treat, 1956.

Dick, Ma, Jude, Dave, Sal, and I returning from our trip to Florida during Christmas break, 1956.

Parliamentarian, Bill Harris; Secretary, Dick Demerly; President, Ed Demerly; Advi
r, Mr. Potier; Vice President, Gerald Sayles; Treasurer, Bob Davis; Reporter, Dave Arnol

FFA boys 1959. Dick and I are seated together.

Gathering with our Graves cousins. Front row: Dick, Ed, Dave, and Scott. Middle row: Sal, Jude, and Janet. Back row Uncle Walt, Aunt Vivian, Ma, and Pa. About 1950.

ROTC summer boot camp training, Ft. Riley, Kansas, 1962.

Ma pinning on my second lieutenant bars, December 1963.

College graduation, December 1963.

Angela in 1974 at the orphanage in Seoul, South Korea.

Angela and Dave, 1981.

In the army, 1965.

Cliff climbing in Ranger training, 1965.

Dick, Sal, Jude, and I ready for church in the early 1960s.

Tom and Liz Brown (Martha's sister), Martha and I river rafting, 1986. You can see who's taking this seriously.

Finishing a race, 2011.

Zip lining in Costa Rica, 2019.

Hunting trophies.

First Years

8

Almost A Saint

The following piece was written at the request of a friend who intended to put together a book about the saints among us. He had asked friends and acquaintances to write about someone they knew personally who seemed to live a saintly life.

She wasn't a Catholic. Although a Baptist in her youth, she wasn't a practicing Baptist in my youth. In those years, she very rarely attended worship services other than the baptism of five of her children on December 14, 1952, or an occasional wedding or funeral. She married three times. Nevertheless, I consider her a most holy person.

My mother, Dorothy, was born before women had the vote and passed away a few months before the attack on the Twin Towers. She grew up during the Great Depression, gave birth to most of her children during World War II, saw television inserted into family life, rejoiced during the Civil Rights movement, opposed the Vietnam War, and saw the growth of prosperity in America.

She was the daughter of a small-town lawyer and an elementary school teacher, yet she married a non-church-affiliated, poor farmer at the age of nineteen and had five children by the age of twenty-seven. She and my dad struggled to make a go of a 120-acre farm that had been purchased at a foreclosure sale. They lived in a converted granary with one faucet, an outdoor toilet, and a wood-burning kitchen stove. They started out with half a dozen dairy cattle, a few chickens, and a team of horses.

Although she rarely went to church, she did teach her children Christianity at an early age at nap time on the front room floor using books of Bible stories from the Old and New Testaments. When I, the second child, was about nine, a new retired neighbor stopped one day to ask if he and his wife could pick up all five of us on Sundays for church and Sunday school at the local rural Methodist church two miles away. I think both of my parents were delighted for different reasons. Ma wanted our faith established, but Pa was probably thinking, "Great! There will be some peace and quiet in the house for a while, and the Sunday noon meal will be on time."

Blessed are the poor in spirit. Ma was poor and spirited. She found moments of silent time to read scripture and often sang old hymns while patching piles of jeans and overalls, hanging lots of laundry, butchering chickens, canning vegetables, or making desserts for charity events. One of her favorites was:

Blessed assurance, Jesus is mine!
Oh, what a foretaste of glory divine!
Heir of salvation, purchase of God,
Born of His Spirit, washed in His blood.

Refrain:
This is my story, this is my song,
Praising my Savior all the day long;
This is my story, this is my song,
Praising my Savior all the day long.

And:
Bringing in the sheaves,
Bringing in the sheaves,
We will come rejoicing,
Bringing in the sheaves.

And another:
Work for the night is coming,
Work through the morning hours;
Work while the dew is sparkling,
Work 'mid springing flowers;
Work when the day grows brighter,
Work in the glowing sun;
Work for the night is coming,
When man's work is done.

She taught us simple bedtime prayers and made sure we understood the real meaning of Christmas and Easter. On Sunday afternoons, she'd ask us what we'd learned at Sunday school and what the sermon was about that morning. She negotiated with Pa so that we didn't have chores on summer mornings during the two-week vacation Bible school. The Sunday school had children's programs at Christmas, Easter, and Mother's Day at which we'd all be given Bible verses to memorize and recite. Ma delighted in helping us memorize our pieces and usually went to the programs without Pa.

Ma's needs were minimal. Offering a eulogy at Ma's funeral, my wife related a story that typified Dorothy. Prior to one of Ma's birthdays, my wife had asked her what she'd like for her birthday. "Oh, you don't have to get me anything," Ma replied. My wife suggested, "How about a sweater?" "No thanks," Ma said, "I already have one."

Dorothy never had to feign humility. She lived it. When I was in 6th grade, our class spent part of every school day for several weeks preparing a Mother's Day "tea" program. We designed cards, wrote poems, rehearsed songs, sent invitations, memorized short "pieces," created small favors as gifts, planned for table flowers, and practiced manners for greeting and seating our guests. Weeks before the event, Ma explained that it was very unlikely that she could go since it was spring plowing time and while we were in school, she spent much of her time helping Pa in the fields.

As I left home that morning, Ma said that it looked like a good day for field work and that I shouldn't expect her. The afternoon tea was quite spectacular. The mothers wore pretty hats and gloves and jewelry and sipped their tea most delicately while appreciating our program. About twenty minutes into the event, another mother arrived. She wore no gloves, hat, or jewelry and seemed unusually dark-complexioned. For a moment, I didn't recognize my mother since I hadn't expected to see her there. Then I felt ashamed. She had momentarily interrupted our program, and all eyes were turned toward her. Did they all see what I saw, a plain darkly-tanned farm wife showing up late? I stood to greet her and to lead her to a chair near the back of the room. Because she had not made a reservation, there was not a place card or a table setting for her. Nevertheless, she seemed to relax and enjoy the remainder of the program.

When the other mothers left at the conclusion of our tea, Ma remained for half an hour until school was dismissed. She explained to me that some farm equipment had broken down and that Pa had used the car to go to get parts, so she decided to catch the noon school bus as it passed our farm after taking kindergarten students home; thus, she needed to take the school bus home with us. I was further embarrassed and sulked in one of the rear seats, but my brothers and sisters were delighted to see her and sit with her, and other children on the bus seemed to find it exciting to have her there. At that time, I didn't appreciate the special effort and love my mom demonstrated by this simple act.

Ma had a generous, happy heart. She enjoyed the company of people of all races and religions, all economic levels, all political affiliations, all ages. Our community did not have Asians or African Americans, but when I brought non-white acquaintances home from the military or from my Peace Corps village in Malaysia, Ma seemed to consider it a special honor to have them in her home. She much admired Dr. Martin Luther King. People who knew her well discovered that she wasn't too fond of Harry Truman, so they loved to gently harass her about that though she, with good humor, laughed along with them. I think her dislike for Truman was primarily because he had defeated Thomas Dewey, who had graduated several years earlier from the same high school as she did.

Ma was a caretaker. Naturally, as any mother would, she was my primary company during my year of near isolation when I was bedridden with rheumatic fever at the age of fourteen. After my dad died suddenly at the age of fifty-four, she mourned silently while caring for a long-time friend who was dying of cancer. Her second husband's left arm was amputated just below the elbow following a farm accident when he was seventeen. She felt privileged to be able to help him open containers, tie things, cut food on his plate, etc. When he had recurring cancer and chose not to take treatment, she lovingly cared for him for over a year as he slowly died. They were together for twelve years. Her third husband lived to be ninety-nine. She was his caretaker also nearly until his death despite recovery from her own heart attack and a quadruple bypass. They were together ten years.

Blessed are those who mourn. Ma mourned the loss of her parents, three husbands, a brother and sister, four grandchildren, a daughter-in-law, and many lifelong neighbors and friends.

Ma loved her five children and was always proud of every one of them in the ways they used their talents to succeed and to help others — one a gifted artisan and construction foreman, another a college teacher, another son a very successful farmer on the same farmstead where we were all raised, a secretary who worked for a congressman and ran a personal sewing business while her five children were young, and another who also owns a seamstress business and does some foreign missionary work. But most important is that all of her children and most of her grandchildren and great grandchildren have strong religious faith and are active in their various churches. Two of her children are Roman Catholics, one a Calvinist, one a Baptist, and one a Methodist. Many of the grandchildren maintain the faith of their parents; others have joined evangelical communities.

9

Remembering Pa

10 Questions

What smells do you associate with your father?
Mennan after shave, fresh air, the barn

When you picture your father, what one or two details stand out for you?
hardworking, innovative, self-disciplined

What was your father's favorite thing to eat? To drink?
meat and potatoes, unfrosted yellow cake with milk poured over it, pineapple sundaes, coffee

What was your father's favorite word or phrase or saying or joke?
"Get at it!" "Pipe down!"   "Go get me ..."
"Half the job is getting started." "Get busy!"
"Do the job right the first time, and you won't have to do it twice."

If your father were an animal, what animal would he be?
a workhorse

What specific songs or music did your father listen to, dance to, whistle, or sing while you were growing up?
Country music: Hank Williams, Patsy Cline, Jim Reeves, Ernest Tubb, Eddie Arnold, even the young Dollie Parton. The song "Four Walls" was a perpetual tune in his head.

If asked to put a hand on the part of your body where your father wounded you, where would you place it?
My head, but it's long healed.

If asked to put a hand on the part of your body where your father blessed you or where you wish your father would bless you, where would you place it?
My head

If you had to choose one item or object to symbolize your father, what would you pick?
A tractor or his tool shop

Three Lists

List #1: "Ten Things I Did to Win My Father's Love."

Obeyed his rules

Did well in school

Shut up at the dinner table

Kept quiet when he was around

Kept the radio turned down

Did chores punctually and well

Cleaned my plate

Tried not to spill milk at the table

List #2: "5 Things I Carry of my Father's Shadow." By "shadow" here, I mean inherited or adopted traits or behaviors of your father that you judge to be negative.

Avoiding confrontation?

List #3: "5 Things I Carry of my Father's Gold." By "gold" here, I mean inherited or adopted traits or behaviors of your father that you judge to be positive.

Do the job right the first time

Get it done on time

A husband role model

Interest in crops and animals

Diligence

Modesty

Two Prompts

Prompt #1: "Pa, I remember _____ "

Your cursory glance at my report cards

Your booting me in the behind when I complained while raking stones out of the new yard before planting grass seed

Your pride in things accomplished: new house built from our own timber, walks through wheat fields ready for harvest, new car or farm machine, etc.

Your cutting your fingers in the buzz saw with the last branch to be cut and how the strange smile turned to shock.

Fishing in Canada

Your holding Todi, the St. Bernard,
on your lap

Your rolling Bull Durham cigarettes

Your mysteriously getting a hitch in your
back on days scheduled for hay baling or
stone picking

All seven of us at the drive-in movies in our
small Ford

Your feeling too proud to let us trick or treat
because you wouldn't have your kids
"begging"

Your being in church for my baptism when
I was eleven — the only time I remember
seeing you in church except when you helped
the men prepare fish dinners during Lent

Your tanned lower arms and face, but white
forehead where your weather-worn baseball
cap kept the sun away

Your spitting tobacco out the car window
(and accidentally into the back seat where
we kids were)

Your reading the Sears catalog in your
recliner

Your clicking your false teeth

Your jiggling your dangling foot when you
crossed your legs

Your whistling "Four Walls" while you
worked in your shop

Your carrying me to and from the car for
doctor's visits when I had rheumatic fever

Your bringing me a German shepherd pup
just like Rin Tin Tin

Your tolerating my silliness over rock music, white buck shoes, The Hit Parade, and
American Bandstand

Your letting me read the map and eat in
restaurants on our trip to Ohio together

Your enforced patience on Christmas mornings — extra chores, and eating the number
of pancakes to match our age before opening
gifts by noon

A head-on car collision

Camping in a sixteen-foot trailer —
all seven of us

Ice cream after hot days of haying

Your falling asleep in the car while holding
my three-year-old son on your lap on Easter,
a week before your death

Your attendance at my college graduation
when you at last seemed to realize that all
those years added up to something worth-
while

Your "necking" with Ma in the car to Grand
Ole Opry music while we kids swam at
Round Lake

Your favoritism toward Dick and Jude

Your teasing Ma about how she voted

Your getting tickled by Ma's hands inside
your bib overalls

Your accidentally spilling boiling water down
my back

Prompt #2: "Pa, I don't remember _____ "

> Your telling me you were proud of me
>
> Your thanking me for anything
>
> Your touching or holding me (except when you had to carry me when I was sick)
>
> Your crying
>
> Ever seeing you drunk, in fact, hardly ever seeing you drink alcohol
>
> Your helping with any household duties
>
> Your talking about your childhood
>
> Your ever spanking or hitting me
>
> Seeing you pray or doing anything "religious"

"Painting" the Best Memory/Worst Memory of Your Father

Pa, my best memory was the time you treated my older brother, Dave, as an adult. I was a high school senior when Dave returned from Army basic training. So well I remember that evening meal the October day he returned on leave for about a week. In many ways, it was a typical 7:00 p.m. supper after finishing chores. We had pork chops and American fried potatoes, canned corn, and cottage cheese. We five kids sat in our typical positions, and Dave resumed the space he had vacated two months earlier. However, things were different. Instead of the usual conversation between Ma and you while we kids listened and interrupted only to ask for food to be passed, you engaged Dave in conversation as you would an adult guest, not the kid who had left a few weeks ago. At the age of nineteen, Dave was still your "oldest boy," but he was no longer one of the rest of us. And Dave was able to respond like an adult. It was something mysterious and delightful and promising. It seemed to be a rite of passage that I began to look forward to. You asked him about his training and listened thoughtfully as he explained things like bivouac, guard duty, KP, and mail call. You seemed so proud of him, something I'd never seen before when he lived at home and was forever being chastised for blunders and examples he failed to set for the rest of us. You laughed and nodded and continued that conversation long after the chocolate cake dessert, and I sat enthralled by you more than Dave.

I honestly have no worst memories. Perhaps thirty years ago, I had, but my own years of parenting and insight from life experiences have well-tempered what may have been worst memories. There were lots of little moments of bitterness and complaint on my part, but in reality, they were really insignificant.

A Letter to your Father

Hi Pa,

I really wish I could see you now for a while. I sense that you can see me and that you know what my life has been in the forty-nine years since you died. That was over sixty percent of my lifetime ago — far too long. I have seen you in very real dreams, a little more frequently in the first ten years after you died than recently. On all those occasions, you were smiling and so happy to visit with me.

I can imagine how life would be if you were still with us. I know you would be a very best friend in a way you couldn't have been when I was a kid, when you had to be the disciplinarian, the boss, someone determined not to be embarrassed by rude, lazy kids. I thank you for that parenting even though at the time I could never have understood it. I'm glad for the ambitious example you set in your work ethic and for the model you set in being a fine husband. I hope I have emulated that example.

I sensed that new relationship too briefly after I returned from the Peace Corps and married and had a son. But that left us only a couple short years, and I feel cheated when I see other adults with their aging parents. I did have Ma until only twenty years ago, but that's another whole relationship. It's not you and me.

I share your wanderlust. In fact, I still long to visit Alaska just as you wished to. It's the only state I've not been in. If you were here, we'd go together, even to the North Pole!

I wish you could meet my grandkids. Dave's daughter, Brittany, has your determination to succeed, to make something from almost nothing. Like you, she struggled through her childhood, but never let that deter her from her dreams. You never met Angela, but she now has three daughters, the last two twins. I know you'd have loved holding them when they were young in a way that you never held us. Maybe you remember holding Dave when he was three, the two of you falling asleep in the car on Easter Sunday. I wonder if you'd be disappointed in my failures in raising him well. I am. But I'm gradually letting myself realize that there was little I could have done in his adult life to change things. I miss him very much.

You'd probably be disappointed in my divorce after ten years of marriage. I think you really liked Linda. I did too, and I'm not sure even now why our marriage ended. I'm very fortunate to have found Martha three years after the divorce. You'd love her, Pa. And she'd love you. You two would probably resurrect canasta and undoubtedly, you'd have gone bass fishing together. You'd love her stories. She's a great story teller.

I like to think that you and Ma are having a great time together again, laughing and "smooching" and sitting quietly together in confident love for each other.

That's all for right now. I love you, Pa. Thanks for the life you gave me.

Ed

A Letter from your Father to You

Hello Ed,

Though I haven't been with you for nearly fifty years, I've seen what's become of you, and I'm very proud. You are a fine son. Does that sound odd coming from me? I know I never said anything like that to you when you were young. I guess I was just too busy making a living for all of us and trying to have some family fun along the way. Maybe with five kids, it was hard to find you, the second and a really good kid. I suppose Dave got more attention, but then he could be a problem boy, and I needed him to set an example for the rest of you.

I think you realize now that I was raised in a different generation when childhood was abbreviated by the Depression. I was the last of thirteen kids, so my perspective on how to be a parent was undoubtedly shaped by those conditions. I hope you can forgive me if those early years seemed sharp.

Did I seem uncaring about your college ambitions? Maybe I was, but thank goodness your mother spoke up. I eventually saw what it was all about and how important it was to you. I only finished eighth grade and thought you could get by well without all that expensive book learning. I think I was wrong in your case.

What are you doing voting Democrat? That I don't get!

I'm glad you took such good care of Ma in those thirty years after I died. I think you probably were her favorite. Thanks for being so accepting of her other two husbands whom I know were very fine men. You treated them like fathers almost as you'd have done with me if I'd been there.

Keep on keeping the Demerly legacy, Ed. You're doing great!

Love,

Pa

A Letter from You to Your Son

My son, Dave, passed away 19 years ago at age 33 from liver failure and hepatitis, the results of years of addiction to alcohol and drugs. I'm including the eulogy I read at his memorial service.

The Day You Died, Dave

The day you died, Dave, was a beautiful June day — except that you passed away.

It was perfect for recalling hour-long walks around the block when you were three — you and I and your tricycle. Every ant crossing the sidewalk needed inspection and every airplane begged your attention. The day was just right for memories of the day twenty-seven years ago that you and I adopted each other and for thoughts of bedtime books with your teddy bear, which, rather than abandon, you eventually kept hidden in the daytime from your sixth-grade friends. It was a good day to think about spontaneous summertime treasure hunts where my thirty notes scattered from the garage to your upstairs bedroom to the basement to the garden used up what had been a boring time — and the treasure? A trip to see Star Wars or Superman or the "real" Spiderman at Tel-Twelve Mall.

June 26th was a splendid day — except that you passed away.

There were fluffy white clouds floating in the blue summer sky, and there were foxglove, and lavender, and daisies blooming in my back yard. It was very much like the day in your childhood when you playfully chased seagulls on the hill beneath the fort on Mackinac Island, carefree and vulnerable. Or like a day in the park across the street from our place in Australia when you were learning to ride your hard, rubber-tired, two-wheeled bike across the bumpy grass, fun and fearless. It reminded me of many warm days in your childhood, those long, endless days at Summer-Stephens public pool, your young muscles glistening as you dived and swam and laughed in a world meant for fun.

Your farewell day was a superb day —
except that you passed away.

It was a great day for remembering your proud stance while playing your saxophone with the school band marching down Michigan Avenue on Memorial Day or you in your macho manner lugging home your football gear in junior high — the gear weighing as much as you did — or showing off at parents' night that huge papier-mâché tiger you made for a fifth-grade project or anticipating with great excitement your sister's arrival in Chicago, April 22, 1975. It was pleasant for thoughts of John McDonald, who because of a brain injury couldn't play much outside, so it was often your compassion that invited him to play GI Joe or the Guns of Navarone or Star Trek on our screened sun porch. Other days you were with Billy Brackett, Kevin Borso, Alan Siwarski, or Chris Rinna doing things like ringing doorbells and running to hide, racing bikes, or setting up tents and obstacle courses in the back yard. Summer days lived to the fullest!

That Wednesday was a fine day —
except that you passed away.

It was perfect for reminiscing about canoeing down the Rifle River or tenting at just about every state park in Michigan or mountain climbing in the Smokey Mountains (you always ahead of the rest of us and always standing courageously on a daring precipice). There was your painted-on clown face at Disney World, the pandas in Washington D.C., our race down the Washington Monument (you won, naturally), the diorama you were fascinated with at Gettysburg, a blackout in New York City (so without elevators, we had to walk our schnauzer, Charlie, up and down 27 flights of stairs — easy for you), collecting amethyst at a quarry in Canada (you acting like a jewel thief with your pockets loaded), a three-week Western trip where at last you got to do some of the driving, even in hilly San Francisco. Wherever we ran into PACMAN, especially in Las Vegas, you wanted to take me on, knowing that you had the thing memorized and that I was a spastic wreck playing that game. As usual, you didn't want to miss a thing on that trip — not even Elvis's motorcycle at a South Dakota tourist trap.

*That June day was a delightful day —
except that you passed away.*

It was ideal for memories of your compassion for pets — Charlie, Frosty, Sunshine, the rabbit you got at the Eastern Market, and many other cats and dogs you had with Brittany and Eric. It was a perfect day for thoughts of your T-ball practice, gymnastics, and baseball games at Tiger Stadium. You always wanted to sit behind first base to root for Jason Thompson. You loved fishing with your grandpa and at Blue Lake. And every fall, you absorbed football on television. I never did get you to a Michigan State game. That day was nice for remembering your money-making projects — your Dearborn Press and Guide route, bundling a station wagon full of old papers and magazines to haul into Detroit to sell, your toy resale table during the Edison Street fair, lawn mowing, and car washing. You loved to eat and to order the exotic — frog legs and octopus, rabbit and squid, all kinds of curry and other ethnic foods. On our trip out west, I had boasted that in three weeks, I would get you and Angela sick of McDonald's French fries. At our last stop before reaching home, you asked to stop at Micky D's for fries!

June 26th was a spectacular day — except that you passed away.

It was a fine time to remember your favorite holidays — Halloween and April Fool's Day. Were you ever too old to trick-or-treat? You took first prize for your homemade costume in fifth grade — Klinger, from the TV show MASH. I think you liked being tricked more than doing the tricking on April Fool's. You were really tickled to see dog food pour out of the cereal box or to find stones in your shoes or your underwear drawer put in upside down. In the fall, you loved going to Grandma Demerly's farm to pick apples and walk holding "hands" with Grandpa's hook (his artificial hand). And in winter, I taught you to ski at Mt. Brighton, but by the end of the day, you were teaching me with your reckless downhill speed, a part of your lifestyle. You were rightly proud to get your GED and to enroll in college classes. You were nervous and excited to show me your first college English paper, a B+ I think, one about the difficulties of finding your way into college, and difficult they were. In fact, you seldom found the easy path in life. That Wednesday brought thoughts of your love for rock music — Steely Dan, The Who, Kiss, AC/DC, Pink Floyd, and The Doors. The Rolling Stones' concert at the Silverdome was probably your first glimpse of what you'd like heaven to be. Can you forgive me for, after listening to your tapes for several hundred miles across upper Michigan, pulling up to the tollbooth at the Mackinac Bridge and singing loudly to the attendant, "We want the world and we want it now!"?

That day seventeen days ago was a very special day — except that you passed away.

It was great for seeing you with Brittany and remembering the unique joy you felt becoming a father and how you told me at a hamburger joint in Jackson that you wanted to be a dad just like me and how I was thinking that you could do much better than I did. You loved holding her and taking her with you whenever you could, and you worried about spoiling her. You used to get down on the floor with Erik and Brittany when you played with them — and you made play fun. It was a good day for recalling your gratitude and many good intentions: "Thanks a lot, Dad. I'll pay you back as soon as I get my next check." "This really means a lot to me, Dad. Tell Martha thanks too. Any time you need some help in the yard, give me a call." "You don't know how much this helps out, Dad. I know I still owe you from the last time, but I'll make it up to you." And I know how much you meant to and wished you could have, Dave.

Dads aren't supposed to be at their sons' funerals. It's just not the way things are meant to be. But you lived a long life in a short time, son, and once again, you got there first.

The day you died, Dave, was a beautiful June day — except you passed away.

10

My Brief Military Life

The one-way bus ticket from home in Owosso to military life in San Antonio, Texas, was $38.90. It was a stormy March day, so by the time the Greyhound bus arrived at the terminal in St. Louis, Missouri, we were delayed for most of a day waiting for the blizzard to let up before heading to Texas. Although I had planned to arrive a day before I was to report for duty, with this delay, I worried about being AWOL on my first day in the army. I did arrive on time at 11:00 a.m. on March 11, 1964.

Above all, for me, the army was welcomed liberation from the life I had known. I was nearly 3,000 miles away from anyone who knew me or knew my past. I had no baggage to carry, so to speak. I wasn't Shirley's son, the farm boy. I wasn't the serious Methodist choir boy who never missed a Sunday service. I wasn't the college graduate who made no new friends during four years of college. I wasn't a wimpy non-athlete. I wasn't a guy who hardly ever dated. I was simply one of nearly eighty young lieutenants reporting for officer training in the Army Medical Service Corp. I could become a new me.

I longed for this adventure — a destination where everything was new. I had never been out west, and as a student of American history, it was exciting to be stationed in San Antonio, home of the Alamo and in Texas, the home state of Lyndon B. Johnson, the president at the time. I was very ready to put college academics aside for a long while. This was my first genuine experience with broad racial/ethnic integration. The army seemed to do it right. I met Native Americans, Latinos, Blacks, Asians, and Whites — all in the same program with equal opportunities and responsibilities. It was also my first regular and dependable monthly income, and fortunately, I had no real expenses since housing, clothing, medical care, and meals were all provided.

This three-month training assignment seemed to pass quite instantly. Much of it was classroom instruction regarding administrative decision making within the Medical Service Corps, appropriate officer behavior in supervising enlisted men, field training in medical evacuation and triage, physical training, and parade practice. Two incidents I remember well. Soon after lunch on a hot afternoon in a crowded room without air-conditioning while watching film footage of triage of casualties from the Korean War, I passed out. I wasn't alone. These were not actors with simulated injuries and Hollywood makeup. They were servicemen with serious injuries and unbearable pain and medical personnel working frantically to treat them. And I thought I was up to this? What was I doing in the Medical Service Corps? A more amusing incident occurred when I was on nighttime guard duty during field training. Standing alone on the perimeter of the bivouac area, I felt something quite heavy smash against my ankle. I looked down to see an armadillo scurrying away. An enemy ambush?

I went with others on several weekends into San Antonio to movies at a very majestic old theater with a full balcony. I had not gone to movies very often — old free black and white cowboy and comedy shows in Morrice where we sat on outdoor benches and the drive-in movies in the summer with my family and just a few films in Owosso as a teenager and college student.

Thus, even this activity was for me a new adventure. 1963-4 was a time for major releases like *El Cid, Hud, Tom Jones, Giant, The Birds,* and *Two Women.* I saw them all. I also visited the Alamo, and attended the Cinco de Mayo parade. I much enjoyed the ethnicity of this celebration but was surprised to see the Texas governor, John Connelly, riding in an open-air limousine just six months after he was injured in the same motorcade in which President Kennedy was killed.

Although I had preferred an overseas assignment, I had orders to report to the Sixth Army Hospital at Fort Ord in Monterey, California, the basic training center for all the west coast. I arranged to ride from San Antonio with another officer who was assigned to Fort Ord. With a couple weeks before reporting for duty, we took our time traveling across Texas, New Mexico, and Arizona. I saw all of desolate west Texas with its buzzards and cactus and huge, bleak-looking ranches with scrawny cattle. We stopped overnight at Fort Bliss in El Paso, where Dave had been in the army and walked into Juarez. What I most remember about Juarez is the vast gap between the rich and the poor with no apparent middle class — lots of beggars and in open sewer drainage canals, dead dogs and trash.

Passing through New Mexico and Arizona and the Mohave Desert, we drove through Indian reservations on our way to Los Angeles, where we stayed two days with a friend who worked at Capitol Records recording studios. He arranged for us to sit in on a Barbra Streisand recording session just as she was becoming a recognized star. However, when we arrived at the studio, her session had been postponed, so we saw an old country star, Russ Morgan, instead — fascinating, nevertheless. This small-town farm boy found himself at 20th Century Fox and Warner Brothers studios, at the Hollywood Bowl, on Hollywood and Vine, in Beverly Hills touring the homes of the stars, and at Grauman's Chinese theater with the sidewalk with the hand and footprints of Marilyn Monroe. Imagine!

We arrived at Fort Ord on May 13th three days before I had to report, so I had time to familiarize myself with the post, the hospital, Carmel, San Jose, and Monterey. That Saturday was Armed Forces Day with a military parade, speeches, and civilian guests. In the evening, the hospital held a cocktail/buffet/dinner dance party where I began to meet people that I'd be working with.

The hospital was a sprawling, one-floor World War II wooden structure with very long aisles connecting the various wards. There were four of us new 2nd lieutenants being assigned to the hospital, so we were interviewed separately by the various commanding officers of the administrative branches. A few days later, I was assigned to the Plans and Operations office which required a security clearance. My office located in the front of the hospital was featured in a Steve McQueen film, *Soldier in the Rain,* a few years before

I arrived. I couldn't exactly fill his shoes now, could I?

My commanding officer, Colonel Charles Overbay, was, I gradually learned from others, regarded as a demanding, temperamental bully. The other 2nd lieutenants were very relieved to learn that they didn't get stuck with him. Nevertheless, he and I came to respect each other and developed a good working relationship, but I was always much more at ease when he was out of the office. Perhaps it helped that the assistant hospital commander, Col. Overbay's boss, soon learned that his wife and I were both from Owosso, so I had an ally of sorts.

Just what did a Plans and Operations lieutenant do at an army hospital during the Cold War? Primarily, my job was to plan, conduct, and evaluate training drills of all sorts for personnel assigned to the Sixth Army Hospital — doctors, nurses, medics, and administrators. Training included periodic target practice, medical triage, map reading, field hospital setup and operations for the 12th Evac MASH hospital, emergency alert drills, physical fitness, security against subversion and espionage, and chemical/biological/radiological training (gas mask drills). Additionally, I was a security officer (handling classified deployment orders for medical personnel being sent to Vietnam, administrative officer of the day (periodic twenty-four-hour duty as the only administrative officer in the hospital during off hours in the evening and on weekends), hospital inspector on Saturday mornings, officer to verify cash accounts in the financial office and narcotics inventory in the pharmacy, solicitor of contributions to the Army Emergency Relief Fund and for the Kennedy Library Fund, evaluator of field exercises for the MASH hospital, and a courts martial officer.

I had other miscellaneous duties as they arose. I served as a witness at verbal reprimands of enlisted corpsmen. On a couple occasions, I investigated and wrote up reports in response to congressional inquiries. These were initiated whenever a soldier assigned to the hospital had written his or her congressman with a complaint against the army. One complaint was of racial discrimination; another of denied psychiatric treatment. I served on seven or eight courts martial, primarily for being AWOL, but one for insubordination to an officer and another for larceny. If found guilty, the penalty was usually a reduction in rank which also meant a reduction in pay, a written reprimand in the soldier's record, denial of some privileges, and/or assignment of extra duties. More serious matters would have required higher ranking officers as judges. I usually tried to be lenient for first-time offenders. One other common responsibility was to draft letter responses to correspondence for Col. Overbay's signature.

As Administrative Officer of the Day, a duty that occurred about twice a month, I was expected to report for my usual day's work, then stay on duty overnight at the hospital near the emergency room and report for work as usual the following day — over thirty hours without sleep. Sometimes Col. Overbay would allow me to take half of the second day off. There was a small room with a cot near the emergency room, and if we were lucky on a quiet night, we were allowed to sleep but to be awakened should a need arise. Even on quiet nights, we were expected to give orders to the hospital personnel on guard duty, patrol all the wards, and submit a written report on the night's activities. Emergency room patients came with broken bones, car accident injuries, domestic violence injuries, severe internal pain, drug overdoses, attempted suicide, stabbing and gunshot injuries from bar brawls and fights, etc. It was the first time I witnessed death, that of a soldier in a car accident. The car had rolled over him. I had never been to even a family funeral. If a doctor asked, I made first calls using a scripted format to the next of kin regarding death or hospitalization. Fortunately, doctors who treated the casualties usually preferred to make the calls themselves. In this car accident case, I had to verify that all the correct papers were available, filled out accurately, and signed — report of the accident, report of death, death certificate, appropriate notification to his commanding officer, and a detailed list of items removed from the body.

In my first year at the hospital, there was a serious outbreak of contagious meningitis among basic training recruits. Ultimately, within about six months, 109 soldiers died before the post was closed to basic training. Many more were infected but recovered. It was my office in coordination with the hospital commander's office (himself a doctor) and the chief nurse's office that organized a major filmed national two-day conference at the hospital. Both civilian and military doctors were invited to find causes and resolutions to this local epidemic. My role included supervision of setting up charts, photos, and other visual materials, greeting "dignitaries" at the airport and arranging their transportation to and housing at the post, serving miscellaneous needs at the conference, and writing appreciation letters after the conference.

In my second year at Fort Ord, there were severe floods in northern California near Ukiah and near Eugene, Oregon. Our 12th Evac MASH hospital was mobilized to go to that area to set up a tent hospital to treat casualties. I was one of three officers assigned to that convoy to help supervise the mission. Fortunately, by the time we arrived, the floods had abated, and we were dismissed to return to Fort Ord. It was a nice trip, nevertheless.

Regarding my security clearance and the issuance of orders for medical personnel to report for duty in Vietnam, I once blundered. These orders were labeled "SECRET" because at the time, the general public was kept unaware of the degree of non-combat support the US was offering South Vietnam as our military involvement became more and more entrenched. One of our nurses received orders, and in my office, she was given instructions to speak to no one about her orders until given permission to. The next weekend, there was an informal officers' party at the home of one of the lieutenants — just a group of friends. One of my friends worked in the personnel office and also had a clearance since he drafted final orders. I mentioned privately to him that this particular nurse had received orders. He hadn't yet heard that. Early the following Monday, the nurse called our office considerably upset and asked if she could see Col. Overbay and me immediately. Secret matters could not be discussed over the phone. I instinctively knew what was upsetting her. Before she arrived, I hurriedly explained to Col. Overbay that I had breached security regulations and had inadvertently mentioned her orders to the personnel officer. Suddenly, she was at the office door. She reported to Col. Overbay in his closed office though I could hear the gist of their conversation. She thought she was in serious trouble because another officer had discovered that she had orders for Vietnam, but she was certain that she had said nothing to anyone. Col. Overbay calmed her and reassured her that she need not worry. After she left, I waited for the other boot to drop. Col. Overbay called me into his office, and for once, he responded with reserve. He helped me understand how serious my blunder was, that it could be a court martial offense, but that he wouldn't pursue it any further. He trusted that I would be considerably more cautious in the future. And indeed, I was!

While my work in the army was primarily an eight-to-five office job, I did have a considerable amount of time off duty after work and on weekends. This was wonderful leisure with a regular income for the first time in my life. I spent time with officer friends, doctors and nurses, and Red Cross workers I had gotten to know. During lunch breaks, we played table tennis tournaments and pool in the hospital rec room. On weekends and after work, some of us played tennis, had dinners at the officers' club, went to movies at the post theater, searched for starfish and otters and watched whales from Monterrey Bay harbor, relaxed on the beach at Carmel, and had pizzas and beers on Cannery Row and at private parties — mostly at the homes of married officers.

I also did a little volunteer work and traveled up and down the California coast — to Big Sur, Hearst Castle, Los Angeles, San Diego, Tijuana (Mexico), Yosemite for skiing in April, San Francisco, and to San Jose a number of times to visit my uncle Roger Wilson's family and my cousin Robert Demerly's family. I taught middle school Sunday school classes at the post Protestant chapel and served as sponsor for the post's Explorer Scouts SCUBA club though I knew nothing about SCUBA diving. My role was primarily to support their fund-raising activities and to offer them publicity.

My personal life changed during these years. I voted for the first time in a presidential election, spent my first Christmas away from home, first flew in a jet (from Lansing to San Francisco), gambled ten cents in a Reno slot machine, attended my first Catholic mass while traveling with a fellow officer, and bought my first new car — a 1965 green and white, vinyl-top Mustang with red-striped sidewall tires and white vinyl interior. I ordered it with Pa's help to be delivered to the dealership in Owosso where I picked it up when I was on leave. Jude rode with me across the northern states with stops at Mt. Rushmore, the Badlands, Yellowstone National Park, Reno, San Francisco, and San Jose before reaching Fort Ord.

I read lots of novels, plays, and poetry that I hadn't read in college — Eugene O'Neill, Ezra Pound, Sinclair Lewis, Theodore Dreiser, William Faulkner, and everything by John Steinbeck since I was living in his neighborhood, nearby Salinas Valley.

After the first few months in a bachelors' officers' quarters "apartment", I moved to what had been nurses' housing, small individual homes near the hospital. There I adopted a cat that I named Ho Chi Minh. I didn't own a television, but I listened to the radio and to music on a portable stereo I'd bought at the PX. I started drinking coffee and occasionally a little beer. I tried all kinds of ethnic foods — plentiful in California: Chinese, Mexican, Korean, Japanese. I got my first (hard) contact lens. They were a *pain* in dusty field conditions, but I was so proud to not have to wear thick-lens glasses. In a little spare time, I tried to teach myself Spanish and typing and started weight lifting and running regularly. And for several months, I dated the comptroller's civilian secretary from Castroville, the artichoke capital of the world. I experienced a California earthquake, really just a tremor. I was seated in a restaurant booth in Monterey when a really heavy guy plopped down in the seat behind me causing, I thought, my bench to shake, but in fact, the whole restaurant was shaking for a few seconds. I was amused by some military terms — periodic *Hail and Farewell* parties for officers arriving and departing assignments at the post [also called *Hi and Bye* parties], a secret operation called *High Heels*, and *Belles and Bars* dances at the officers' club — bars, meaning lieutenant and captain insignia.

In my weekly work routine, I found my job in the army dull. I'm thankful that we weren't at war, but during peacetime with a military draft, it seemed the army had far too many men during this conflict called the Cold War and far too little for them to do other than to monotonously train and train again. Out of boredom and to make my two years pass faster, I looked for military training opportunities that would take me away from my regular assignment at Fort Ord for a while. I took a couple short courses on base. A slight scar on my right forearm still reminds me of the course in chemical, biological, and radiological warfare. To truly experience the effects of blister gas, each man in the course was administered a pinpoint-sized drop of this gas on his arm. Within a day, the painful blister was the size of a dime. Imagine how incapacitating that would be if sprayed by air onto a company of men in combat! Another course focused on training to serve as a judge on court martial trials.

Perhaps proof that I was desperately bored or young and foolish or both is that I applied for and was accepted for the three-week airborne training course at Fort Benning, Georgia. Because of my poor eyesight, at first, I didn't qualify, but I had gotten to know one of the hospital's ophthalmologists well enough that he had no hesitation in adding his view that my eyesight would qualify. I passed the physical fitness test which in part included running a mile in combat boots in less than ten minutes. My time was six minutes and forty-five seconds.

I reported at Fort Benning on a Saturday, October 3, 1964, so I had the weekend to unpack and explore the post, but we were already into rigorous training on Monday. I liked the fact that all insignia was removed from our uniforms so we were never aware of who were privates, sergeants, and officers. After some administrative details and distribution of equipment and some physical training, we practiced exiting the plane exercises from three-foot platforms. One major goal of the training, it seemed to me, was to weed out weaklings during the first week. We had nearly three hours of running, rope climbing, crawling, daily dozen exercises, etc. before breakfast! After more plane exit practice and landing practice from a six-foot platform, we climbed up a thirty-four-foot tower in our parachute harnesses which at the door of the tower were attached to a zip line. This was additional practice to perfect our exiting the plane. This one exercise eliminated a number of men who froze in the doorway and just couldn't jump. We spent time learning to collapse our chutes after landing so that we wouldn't be dragged across an open space or visible to enemy forces after landing. The rest of the week was more of the same, but already members of our units were disappearing — either quitting, injured, or being dropped from the program, so it was my huge relief to survive the first week.

After the weekend off, Monday's training was especially brutal. This time I lacked six inches of reaching the top of the thirty-foot rope climb. Most of the week was filled with longer runs, instruction on packing parachutes though we didn't pack our own chutes, and practice jumps from a 250-foot tower with packs and equipment as we improved our steering skills. This tall tower had four arms at the top, and suspended from each arm was a cable with a modified parachute attached. We were harnessed to the chute and pulled to the top of the tower which then released us into free fall with our chutes. We repeated this exercise a number of times. It was almost like an amusement park ride. In a mock boxcar-like C-130 airplane, we practiced standard procedure for a mass jump — equipment checks, shuffling to the door, and exiting. Having qualified on all the apparatus, I was gaining confidence that I could complete the course. Our platoon won honors as the highest-scoring platoon twice that week.

We were scheduled for our first jump on Monday afternoon of the third week, but the winds were too strong for a first jump, so it was postponed. Instead, we made two jumps on Tuesday even though it was still quite windy. Prior to our first jump, I think we were all overconfident, certain that we had this all down to perfection. We used static lines that automatically opened our chutes, but we counted to ten anyway to be sure we were clear of the plane and to realize that our chutes were open so that we didn't have to use our emergency chutes strapped on our waists. I wasn't prepared for the sudden gush of air caused by the speed of the plane as I exited the door and found that I was upside down until my chute popped opened. Then for a minute or two, we descended from our 1200-foot launch almost like a flock of thirty-six angels. It was a most beautiful, silent, serene view as we floated toward earth steering away from the other eighty chutes so as not to steal their air and cause them to plummet. We had learned not to look down as soon as we anticipated that we were about 100 feet from landing. To avoid the panic of feeling that the ground was racing toward us, we were to relax in our landing mode and look ahead. Our landing site was simply an open field surrounded by forest, so it was important that we all exit the plane at a carefully measured pace so that no one would be landing in the trees. Remember, it was a relatively breezy day, so despite our steering attempts, our chutes did drift, and when we landed, quite a number of us had difficulty collapsing our chutes and were dragged over rough surface. I landed knee-deep in a puddle but had no trouble gathering my chute. Several guys did get injured and were unable to complete the course. I didn't have quite the same naïve surety as we prepared for our second jump that afternoon, but it went much better for all of us with calmer winds.

On Wednesday, we made a morning jump with eighty pounds of equipment and a nighttime jump. Both went very smoothly. While in formation before being dismissed at the end of the day, we had a minute of silence in memory of President Herbert Hoover who had passed away the previous day. On our last jump on Thursday morning, I had the "honor" of being first out the door. This was becoming fun! Nevertheless, we were already finished! I had nearly forgotten that first ten days of torture, and as I saw the new class of potential paratroopers arriving, I felt a particular pride in having done so well. We had a brief "graduation" ceremony where we received our wings insignia, and later that day, Jude and Ma arrived. We had dinner out to celebrate, and the next morning we stayed for a military parade before heading for a short leave in Michigan.

So back to my routine at Fort Ord where Col. Overbay had suspended a packed parachute over my office chair to welcome me back. He was quite sure at this point that I intended to go R.A. — regular army, i.e., to become a career officer. I let him think that though that was far from my thoughts. The same dull routine set in, and soon I was looking for alternatives. I found a possibility — ranger training. That would take me back to Fort Benning for a full five weeks; however, I needed one year of active duty remaining after the completion of the course. It was already January 1965, and my scheduled discharge date was early March 1966. Just how badly did I want to do this? I'd have to re-enlist for an additional six months so that if I were accepted and completed the course by August 1965, I'd have a year of remaining service. I was young and adventuresome, and some would say foolish. It would be a prestigious accomplishment since very few men applied for, let alone completed the course and could wear the Ranger insignia. Perhaps I didn't fully take into consideration that by escaping for five weeks, I'd be adding six more months to my tedium? In June of 1965, I was headed again to Fort Benning. The primary purpose of ranger training is to prepare men to form patrols in wartime and in all types of terrain. These patrols of six to ten men would infiltrate enemy lines to accomplish specific missions — perhaps to detonate ammunition stockpiles, to gather information, to rescue prisoners of war, etc. With our increased involvement in the war in Vietnam, our training was focused on jungle warfare, mountainous conditions, and sneak nighttime beach landings rather than urban conflict or desert warfare associated with later wars in the Middle East.

As in airborne training, our rank was removed so that privates and captains worked as equals. After a week of orientation and pretty severe physical fitness routines, our group of perhaps twenty men were trucked from Fort Benning in west central Georgia to Dahlonega in mountainous northern Georgia where we were to learn cliff climbing and rappelling skills on steep granite rock walls. Today this has become a popular sport at indoor gyms where all the apparatus is prepared. In contrast, we learned how to pound pitons into the rock face, attach snap links, tie slip knots, bowlines, and clove hitches, and ascend and descend chimneys and chutes. We practiced route selection, belaying, tension climbing, and traversing. Most difficult was evacuating casualties while rappelling. Our training started on the ground and on thirty-foot timber walls, but within a few days, we were heading up and down mountainous cliffs. I had climbed up and down the outside of our seventy-foot silo on the farm without any safety protocol using steel steps built into the wall of the silo. That was probably much more dangerous than this where safety was always paramount. Rappelling was almost as fun as parachuting!

For the second phase of training, we were trucked to the Okefenokee swamps in southern Georgia for about ten days of primarily nighttime patrol training in neck-deep swamp water. This, for me and all of us, I think, was the most treacherous part of the course. Before heading into the swamps, we practiced "swimming" in pool water with our fatigue uniforms and combat boots on. That including retrieving items from the bottom of the pool and "rescuing" a classmate by swimming the length of the pool dragging him. One other challenge was to zipline about 100 yards from a forty-foot tower down over a lake, again in full uniform and boots while hanging onto a foot-long horizontal pipe. The far end of the zipline was anchored to a huge cement wall. We were expected to drop into the water, but not too soon while we were too high, and certainly not too late. This seemed possible. However, before I plunged into the murky water feet first, nobody told me that I might get stuck in the mud at the bottom of the lake. My boots were firmly held, and I had nothing to grab to help me up. Panic and an urgency for air somehow got me to the surface.

We lived on K-rations and swamp water with iodine pills and slept primarily in short naps during the day when we could find enough high ground. All night, we moved through the swamp to imaginary enemy positions. Using our map and compass skills while huddled under ponchos to hide our flashlights, we rotated command responsibilities to practice the reality of the leader being suddenly killed and another would have to take over to accomplish the mission. The Okefenokee on a moonless night is incredibly dark. Our faces were camouflaged so we could hardly see each other. We used small pieces of reflector tape on the backs of our helmets and were expected to stay within an arm's length of the man in front of us. And for certain, we had to stay as silent as possible. Now assume that you've had essentially no sleep for four days, you're walking chest high in murky swamp water holding your rifle over your head with one hand while trying to stay in touch (so to speak) with the man ahead of you. Add to that the very uneven swamp bottom with roots and weeds and mud. How silent do you think we were?

One of our tasks there was to bargain with imagined local farmers for some produce — onions, carrots, chickens, rabbits, potatoes, etc. The "farmers" were part of our teaching staff. We were given no rations for the day because we were expected to make a stew using the produce and swamp water. And so we killed and defeathered the chickens and skinned the rabbits and chopped up the vegetables, and using our helmets as stew pots, we had a feast! I might mention that part of our training included identifying edible plants and roots and even how, should circumstances ever demand it, how to survive on our own urine and feces. Gratefully, we were never tested on that skill.

We also practiced handling small alligators and large non-poisonous snakes, just so that we might feel at ease should we come upon them. One day during a brief lunch break, we were sitting under small trees and brush when one of the men spotted a non-poisonous snake on a branch in the brush just over his shoulder. Rather than ignore it, he thought he'd show his bravery (and stupidity?) by grabbing its tail and yanking it off the branch. Predictably, it suddenly struck his arm and wouldn't release its bite until one of our trainers helped by squeezing the sides of its jaws. Except for shock and a little bleeding, the ranger-to-be was all right. Lesson learned?

One day we were divided into two patrols some distance apart so that we couldn't see or hear each other. To practice silent, invisible coordination behind enemy lines, we were sent one at a time to take messages to the other team perhaps a half mile away in heavily wooded lowland. We were given the coordinates of their location and using our maps and compasses, expected to find them and return with their information. Off I went quite confident in my map and compass skills. I found the other team with little difficulty, exchanged information, and headed back to my camp. I was fairly certain I remembered the way and carelessly neglected to use my map and compass. Partway back, I realized that I wasn't so certain. I couldn't yell for help. That surely would have disqualified me. I reconnoitered several times and finally (perhaps accidentally?) I could see my team in the distance. That panic almost matched that of the stuck-in-the-mud day.

One late evening while it was still light out, we were moving single-file down a dirt road carrying our packs and weapons. I was really drowsy, but I kept moving one step after another. Suddenly, I started to stumble. I had fallen asleep while walking and had drifted toward a drainage ditch. That clearly awakened me, and I was soon back in formation.

The last segment of our training was at Elgin Air Force base near Valparaiso, Florida, in the panhandle region. Here we practiced nighttime beach landings for infiltration behind enemy lines. Similar to the final week of airborne training, this was almost a time to relax. After training on land, we were brought into the Gulf of Mexico on small ships and practiced descending on netting thrown over the side of the ship where we embarked floating rafts and stealthily paddled them to shore where we established a rendezvous patrol.

I think my success in completing this course was my pure stubbornness, pride, and refusal to quit, perhaps part of my years of growing up on a farm. Pa had always said, "You have to finish the job." He meant getting the cows milked before eating breakfast or supper or the wheat harvested before the rain came. The army meant, "The mission must be accomplished!"

I returned to Fort Ord for another year of service. Col. Overbay was reassigned to South Korea, and Major Emerson replaced him. My relationship with him was much more comfortable. At the same time, I was promoted to 1st Lieutenant and began to focus more on my time off duty. Was I beginning to count the days until discharge? For certain, I was becoming much more aware of the war in Vietnam as orders for reassignment of medical personnel increased. I began to receive personal letters from nurses and other officers

I'd become friends with at Fort Ord who were now serving in Vietnam.

Knowing that I had no intention of remaining in the army, I gave serious thought to what I'd do next. Would I return to Michigan and begin my teaching career? I would have been happy with that choice, but since my college years when Kennedy was president, I was very intrigued by Peace Corps service. I had no personal commitments and no other employment opportunities lined up, so I filled out a lengthy application for the Peace Corps and waited. Weeks later, I received a telegram. Imagine that, a telegram — one of two I received in my lifetime. I was accepted by the Peace Corps to train to be an agricultural worker raising chickens in India. That's a job I felt very qualified for, but I really preferred to teach, so I declined that offer, but reassured them I was still much interested in Peace Corps service as a teacher. Within ten days, I got a second telegram offering me a position as a teacher in Malaysia. After looking on a map to find Malaysia, I accepted. Training would begin in Hawaii at the end of August 1966 just weeks after my discharge on August 11th.

I left the army a year and a half before the United States started to deploy combat troops to Vietnam. I was supposed to continue in the army reserves for another three years with occasional training meetings and annual summer drills at Camp Grayling in Michigan. Although I was registered for reserve duty, I didn't receive any letters requiring my presence at meetings until the summer of 1967 when I was teaching in Borneo. I think my mother forwarded that letter by sea mail, so

I received it weeks later after the summer training had ended. I replied stating my circumstances and was later excused from any further reserve duty.

It seems ironic that while serving in the Army Medical Service Corps, I never rode in a helicopter, the primary mode of medical evacuation in Vietnam. I did ride several times in single-engine, four-seater airplanes. Equally ironic is that I found myself in Saigon in December 1966. The charter flight taking eighty Peace Corps volunteers to Malaysia stopped for refueling there. As we approached the air field (not really an airport), the plane maintained an altitude of over a mile high to avoid ground fire; then suddenly we descended in an almost vertical position to the landing. From the air, we could see areas in the distance where bombs were being dropped. We were allowed to deplane but had to stay inside the terminal. I can still see the vacant faces of soldiers waiting for flights out of Vietnam and the worried looks of those arriving laden with combat gear. After our forty-five-minute stay, we ascended like a rocket, straight skyward for a mile before leveling off.

In retrospect, I'm thankful for military service in a time of relative peace. I'm proud to have had military experience that most men in the generations just before mine had had. I was grateful to list military experience on resumes and thankful for the GI bill, which paid most of my graduate school expenses. I especially appreciated that period as a time of personal growth, a time to establish individual identity and to discover in part who I was and who I was becoming. Strangely enough, I never thought of my service as "serving my country" or "doing my duty". My military time was simply an obligation I had made and one I intended to and felt obligated to complete honorably. Finally, I'm grateful that I will eventually be buried in the beautiful Great Lakes National Cemetery in Holly, Michigan.

⟫⟫ 11 ⟪⟪

Sinking Deep In Sin

An old Methodist hymn titled "Love Lifted Me" had these lines:

I was sinking deep in sin
Far from the peaceful shore
Very deeply stained within
Sinking to rise no more

But the master of the sea
Heard my despairing cry
From the waters lifted me
Now safe am I

Save me, God, for the waters have reached my neck.
I have sunk into the mire of the deep, where there is no foothold.
I have gone down to the watery depths; the flood overwhelms me. (Psalms 69: 1-3)

When I was about nine, a newly retired neighbor stopped one day to ask if he and his wife could pick up all five of us on Sundays for church at 9:00 followed by Sunday school at 10:30 at the Bennington Methodist church two miles away. Up until then, our only religious instruction was children's Bible stories Ma read us at nap time and a simple bedtime prayer.

The small rural church was built in the late 1800s and could seat perhaps 100 people in the old wooden pews which originally had wooden barriers in the pews, I presume to segregate men from women during services or to reserve family pews. A typical service might have had forty of our farm community members in attendance — mostly women — in their Sunday best, hats and sometimes gloves included. Of course, at Christmas and Easter services, there were extra chairs set up in the aisles, but my parents were never in them. I remember both parents in church together only once — when all of us children were baptized on the same day — December 14, 1952.

In my early years as a Methodist, the church had linoleum-tiled floors, a back room behind the altar where small children met for Bible lessons during the forty-to-fifty-minute weekly sermon, a very high ceiling and tall frosted glass windows, a choir balcony which was no longer used as a choir loft but as a Sunday School classroom for high school students, an old upright piano, an elevated pulpit and choir area surrounded by a communion rail, a full basement with a kitchen and tables for funeral lunches, fish fries, wedding receptions, and Sunday School lessons as well as Vacation Bible School, a small steeple with a church bell, and two outhouses. Communion was distributed perhaps three times a year, at first at the communion rail but later in the pews where little cubes of Wonder Bread and a tray of shot glasses filled with grape juice were passed.

Eventually the church raised enough money for renovations — a red center aisle carpet, two simple restrooms, paint inside and out, updated kitchen appliances, and removal of the pew barriers.

We five children were raised as Methodists and very seriously practiced that faith. We seldom missed Sunday services which included the main service followed by Sunday School and then Methodist Youth Fellowship in the evening. Perfect attendance was rewarded with small gifts — perhaps a pin or a bookmark or a small Bible story picture for three or six months of uninterrupted attendance. The award for a year's perfect attendance was a King James Bible with a zipper, white for girls, black for boys. I think all of us except Dave achieved that reward. We memorized Bible passages and recited at Christmas and Mother's Day ceremonies. We attended Vacation Bible School in the summer, sang in the choir, served as candle lighters, and even delivered sermons on Youth Sunday. During those years, I read the Bible from Genesis to Revelation several times, memorized numerous verses, and listened faithfully to Billy Graham sermons on the radio.

That faith remained strong through my college and army years. I taught Sunday school to middle school children at the Fort Ord chapel and worked for several charities. Being a conservative Protestant, I didn't drink or smoke in my early adulthood.

During the last months of my military service, I applied for the Peace Corps. I'm sure that I was influenced by President Kennedy's call to service when he established the Peace Corps during my college years, but at that time, I was already committed to two years of military service. In the summer of 1966 when my military service was nearing its end, I hadn't yet made any specific plans for what would come next, and I wasn't in a relationship that might have conflicted with Peace Corps service, so I applied, thinking that if that was something I really wanted to do, now was the time.

However, I'm sure that my early years in the church were even a greater influence. Missionaries visited the church annually to appeal for donations for their work. As they spoke of their lives in Africa, Central America, and Asia, my imagination put me in those settings serving God in some way. I had also read the works of Thomas Dooley, a medical doctor who died in 1961 and who brought the Catholic faith to the people of Southeast Asia during the 1950s. I was also impressed by Nobel Peace Prize winner, Albert Schweitzer's work in what is now Gabon in West Africa. As a Lutheran theologian and medical doctor, he worked for years establishing a hospital in the interior of Gabon. (I was so impressed that I named my boar Dr. Schweitzer.) Although the Peace Corps would not allow proselytizing, still I could perhaps use my skills as a teacher to help others.

Of course, I was also influenced by wanderlust, probably "inherited" from my parents to a degree and enhanced by my travel through many of the states while I was in the army. My study of and great interest in literature had an impact as well — especially works like Conrad's *Heart of Darkness* and *Lord Jim* and Pearl Buck's *The Good Earth*. There was a little-known singer in the 60s named John Gary who had a rendition of a song from the 40s titled *Far Away Places*. I had one of his albums with that song which sent my mind into a fantasy world.

Faraway places with strange sounding names
Far away over the sea
Those faraway places with strange sounding names
Are calling, calling me
Goin' to China or maybe Siam
I wanna see for myself
Those faraway places
I've been reading about
In a book that I took from the shelf
I start getting restless whenever I hear
The whistle of a train
I pray for the day I can get underway
And look for those castles in Spain
They call me a dreamer
Well maybe I am
But I know that I'm burning to see
Those faraway places with strange sounding names
Calling, calling me

Luckily, I was accepted for Peace Corps training for a position as a teacher in Malaysia, a country that had received independence from Great Britain only three years earlier. At the time, I wasn't certain where Malaysia was. That made it even more appealing.

I wound up as a teacher in a small rainforest village in North Borneo (Malaysia's state of Sabah) four hours by outboard motor up the Labuk River. This village, Sapi by name, had no electricity, no running water (other than the tidal river), no telephones, and no roads, but what it did have was an Australian Anglican mission elementary school and church founded about five years before I arrived. I was there to replace the Australian missionary and teacher of the upper-level classes. I was there only to teach, not to proselytize or promote religion though I did teach weekly Bible lessons as part of the curriculum in this private school. Most of the fifth and sixth grade students had converted to Christianity, but others were Muslims and pagans.

Ironically, it was here that I began to drift away from my faith even though I continued to attend Sunday services. The priest, a native Malaysian who had studied in the United States, invited me on several occasions to travel with him further up the river to remote villages where he introduced Christianity using stories and flip charts with colored pictures of Biblical stories. The entire village attended (perhaps seventy people), sitting on the ground in a palm-leaf covered shelter fascinated by the storytelling for over two hours at a time. I felt almost like one of the original apostles as they spread the gospel to those who had never heard the good news.

After a year with four or five of these visits — a couple of them were return visits — the priest showed me his annual report which he sent to the Australian headquarters from which he was receiving funds for the continued support of his mission. I was stunned and disillusioned. The great emphasis was on the number of converts he had made, numbers which seemed quite inflated. Perhaps it was simply my misunderstanding? At the conclusion of each visit, he asked the villagers to put their thumbprints onto a piece of paper to acknowledge that they had accepted Christ as their savior. How could that be after a brief two-hour story telling? Could they possibly have understood the magnitude of such a decision? Perhaps it was my misunderstanding. The Holy Spirit, after all, works in mysterious ways. Nevertheless, to me it felt fraudulent and hypocritical. I began to waiver in my own faith.

That was undoubtedly the beginning of my "sinking deep in sin". Upon my return to the states, I launched my teaching career, completed my master's degree, got married, taught in Australia, adopted two children, got divorced and remarried, buried my son — all the time with a superficial, half-hearted practice of faith. Both of my wives were Catholics though my non-conversion to Catholicism didn't seem to be an obstacle. When I married my first wife, a Catholic, I began to attend Catholic mass although I didn't convert to Catholicism. For thirty-seven years, my faith faded.

My children were baptized and catechized in the faith. I continued to attend services somewhat regularly. I enjoyed the music and the solitude of church services, and occasionally, a good sermon, but my heart wasn't in it, and my thoughts drifted even further toward disbelief. I remembered being very involved in church activities as a youth, and at this point in my life, I just didn't want to commit to that degree of involvement which I felt was a very necessary element in calling oneself a Christian.

Then in 2007 without the urging of anyone, I enrolled in a seven-month study of the Catholic faith the purpose of which was to join the church at the end of the study. My wife was surprised, but pleased. My daughter's response was, "You, Dad?" My siblings thought that I already was a Catholic since I had been attending church all these years. And my own response? I was skeptical. At the first session, I confessed that I was not at all sure that I would be among those who would join the faith the following year.

Why then did I even sign up for the class? I can only say that for some time I had been longing for the kind of inner peace and certainty in faith that I had known as a teenager and young adult. The influence of those early years was undoubtedly a catalyst all these years later. Furthermore, I recognized the faith and Christian demeanor and service of intelligent people I respected, especially my wife, her father, and my nephew who was a Protestant and an MIT graduate in engineering. There were other friends, colleagues at work, and family members as well who influenced me in positive ways toward this decision simply by the example of their Christian (and even Muslim) lives. Their influence was balanced by atheist and agnostic acquaintances who were also fine people.

Perhaps another impulse was that I was nearing my twenty-fifth anniversary with Martha, and because we were not married in the church and because she is a devout Catholic, I wanted to seek an annulment of my first marriage so that we might marry in the church on our twenty-fifth anniversary. It seemed necessary, logical, and right that I should convert to Catholicism.

Nevertheless, I sincerely questioned whether in "good faith" I could join the church. I had a serious lack of sincere basic belief in God and Christianity. Despite that, I decided to enroll in this class thinking that it might be the best venue to ask questions. The staff and fellow initiates were direct in both their questions and answers without any pressure that I must decide affirmatively by the end of my instruction. They allowed me to make that decision on my own; in fact, they almost insisted that I not join the church with doubt and reservations.

I credit the prayers of many others and my own prayers for my return to faith. Martha's constant, steady support was invaluable. I saw her persistent faith as a model. I recognized that same faith in my RCIA (Rite of Christian Initiation of Adults) sponsor, Glenn O'Kray, among others. At the same time, a discovery of my family European history which included priests and distant family with a strong Catholic faith served in its small way as an influence. I began reading the works of Henri J.M. Nouwen and books about the lives of saints. I recalled homilies of priests I admired including those of Fr. Dan Jones, Fr. Patrick Jankowiak, Fr. Andrew Czajkowski, Fr. Richard Cassidy, Fr. Daniel Trapp, and especially Fr. Eric Weber's reading of the Last Rites at my son's death five years earlier. The Little Blue, Black, and White Books of Bishop Ken Untener were powerful daily influences. They all helped to answer my misgivings about choosing Catholicism when I had great respect for other faiths including those of Protestant sects and Islam.

Today I can only say when people ask, that the Holy Spirit works in mysterious ways, that I felt called to return to God, and that prayer is answered according to God's plan. I, the very skeptical "believer", had been praying for some time regarding my faith, and I expect that a few others might have been as well.

For thirty-seven years, I hadn't asked. I simply hadn't asked.

Then the master of the sea
Heard my despairing cry
From the waters lifted me
Now safe am I

Since that Easter in 2007, I have become very involved in church activities and very fulfilled in my faith. Being a Catholic seems so right for me. My daily routine, my thoughts, my prayers and Bible reading, and my relationships with others are based on my quiet pride in knowing Jesus and being a Catholic. I have attended many Bible studies, taught catechism, served as a lector, sung in the choir, joined the men's fellowship, and led forums dealing with ecumenical and interfaith matters. I've even attended mass in Germany, Australia, France, Cuba, Singapore, Malaysia, Costa Rica, and Vietnam. I've visited St. Paul's Basilica and the Sistine Chapel in Rome, Notre Dame Cathedral in Paris, the Basilica of the National Shrine of the Immaculate Conception in Washington D.C., and Our Lady of Lourdes Grotto in France. Particularly moving was the beatification ceremony in 2017 of Blessed Father Solanus Casey with about 70,000 other Catholics at Ford Field in Detroit. I realize that my faith has much room for growth. I'm confident that growth will continue and hopeful that I can be a good model of Catholicism for all who know me.

Had I remained in my farm community years ago, might I not have wandered so far from the strong faith I had had as a youth?

12

My Pathetic Athletic Life

It's all a rather sorry story. In elementary school, I seldom joined, nor was I very often invited to join, spontaneously-organized playground activities such as Red Rover-Red Rover, tag, softball, tug-of-war, and even snowball fights. If I was coerced because a team lacked one player, I was usually the last one chosen. Instead, I preferred somewhat solitary play on the swings or even, with a few other boys, games with the girls— guessing games, rope high jump, or hide and seek.

At home with my brothers and sisters and occasionally a few neighbors, we made up our own games with names like raggy-baggy and ghost game, both variations of tag. We played softball which we especially enjoyed whenever Ma would join us. In winter, we sledded down the driveway, sometimes for hours, with one sled and as many of us as we could squeeze onto it. We built snow forts, had snowball battles, slid on a small ice pond out in the corn field, played goose chase while waiting for the school bus, and made-up Tarzan-like games on the ropes and hay bales in the barn. In our teens, we acquired a few pairs of ice skates. In summer between planting and harvesting, we took short camping trips to state parks in a small travel trailer. Does that type of camping qualify as a sport?

I had no athletic life in high school other than attending a few basketball games. Because of rheumatic fever in my early teens, I couldn't take gym classes. My brothers and I didn't participate in any school team sports because of our obligation to be home for farm chores after school.

In college, all freshmen and sophomores were required to take physical education classes. Except for volleyball, badminton, and square dancing — not exactly competitive sports, I selected individualized sports like swimming and gymnastics. Not that I was particularly interested in the games or even understood what I was watching, I did attend a few college football and basketball games and gymnastic meets. Never hockey. If precision military drill teamwork counts as a sport, I can say that indeed I did participate in college sports.

The army demanded a bit more physical activity during basic training, airborne training, and ranger training — lots of running, rope climbing, obstacle courses, and the "daily dozen" calisthenics, as well as mandatory chin-ups prior to entering the mess hall. Anyone who couldn't do the required 15 or 20 chin-ups had to go to the end of the chow line.

However, as an officer after I was given my regular assignment at the 6th Army Hospital in Monterey, California, I was exempt from regular physical training though we did need to take semi-annual physical ability tests. It was assumed that officers would be responsible enough to take care of their physical condition on their own. Almost to my surprise and at the invitations of others, I began to find all sorts of athletic recreational activities. I started bowling and playing tennis and continued regularly on a bowling team and played tennis frequently — singles and doubles with fellow officers. During lunch breaks at the hospital, nurses, Red Cross workers, and officers routinely played rounds of table tennis. Was I becoming an athlete after all? I continued to run on an outdoor track just so my physical tests scores would not be too embarrassing, and I began working out with weights. Once, and only once, a fellow officer invited me to hit golf balls with him. We didn't set out to play a round, just to hit a few balls. That's what it was — a few balls, perhaps six or eight before I surrendered. Call it lack of perseverance if you will, but when each ball seemed to turn at a 90-degree angle opposite its planned destination, it all seemed pretty futile. I skied for the first time at Yosemite National Park in April while snow remained on the mountaintops. What a fine time to ski in shorts and T-shirts.

Two parts of my military service — airborne and ranger training — were entirely physical from waking at 4:30 to sleep at 9:00. To be sure, during ranger training, sleep may have on occasion come only every two days. Much of our training in the Okefenokee swamps in Georgia was during nighttime. During the day, with luck, we could fit in a short nap leaning against a tree on a swampy knoll. I recall falling asleep while walking in single file along a dirt path. I awoke as I started to stumble toward a drainage ditch. One two-week segment of our training included cliff climbing and rappelling which has since become much more of what we think of as sport than it ever was then. Although it was in no way skydiving, my six parachute jumps during airborne training might qualify as a segment of my athletic life. Our jumps were from 12,000 feet. The idea was to get to the ground and out of enemy fire as quickly as possible. I didn't hear of skydiving as a sport until years later.

Within a month after leaving the army, I joined the Peace Corps, and so the physical activities that had become quite routine for me while I was in the service faded away for lack of facilities. However, I did find a new adventure. Peace Corps training was on the big island of Hawaii — far from Honolulu and Waikiki Beach, but very near two major volcanoes. One weekend, several of my fellow trainees and I ventured to the top of Mauna Kea, 13,796 feet. Fortunately, it was inactive at the time so we could walk across the crater being careful not to slip into one of a number of huge crevasses that were emitting steam. Fun!

While serving in the Peace Corps in North Borneo, Malaysia, I sometimes joined schoolboys playing barefoot soccer. They didn't have shoes. Other times we played badminton and volleyball on a mud-hardened court or tossed frisbees that my aunt had sent me. I learned how to maneuver a dugout canoe on the fast-moving Labuk River. And again, I found a mountain to scale, Mt Kinabalu, the highest mountain in southeast Asia at 13,455 feet. This was a two-day effort with some high school students — one day up and another day down. We stayed overnight in primitive bunk houses near the summit. What a view from the top — small villages and padi fields and rain forest in the distance.

Upon my return from Malaysia, I fell into years of lethargy while I finished my graduate degree, launched my teaching career, married, and started my family. I can think of only two athletic endeavors during that time. Teaching for a semester in Pentwater, Michigan, a small sand-dune town on the shores of Lake Michigan, I learned to waterski. Perhaps I have waterskied once since then.

I completed my graduate degree at Michigan State University in June 1970 and took a summer job at a boys camp in Ely, Minnesota. There I supervised a cabin of middle school boys and "taught" canoeing and orienteering. Maybe I should say that some of the older boys taught me canoeing, but orienteering I knew well from ranger training. After teaching the boys how to use a compass and a topographical map, the camp director would blindfold three or four of the boys at night, put them in the car with me and drive us to a location I had picked out earlier. At the site, we'd lead them some distance into the woods out of sight of any paths or roads. After the director left and we could no longer hear the car, I removed the blindfolds and we set up pup tents for the night. The next day with only their compasses and maps, they endeavored to find their way back to the boys camp four or five miles away. We always managed to return — eventually. Some groups seemed to go in circles and make a number of turnarounds before feeling certain they were headed home.

In August as the camp closed for the season, four of us counselors and a beagle decided to go canoeing for an eight- day trip on the Turtle River in the Boundary Waters in Canada just north of the Minnesota border. We packed supplies for a ten-day journey into the wilderness. Think of the movie *Deliverance* without murder. We occasionally saw other humans: two native Canadian women harvesting wild rice, several fly-in fishers, and some residents at fly-in fishing lodges. We had no means of communicating with the civilized world and had to keep a certain pace because Canadian park rangers where we had left our car expected us back within about ten days before they'd start a search. We paddled all day whether in hot sun or cold, windy rain. Sometimes we crossed lakes, but mostly we paddled downstream on the Turtle River. We had to carry our canoes and supplies at certain portages around waterfalls. These portages were seldom marked with a sign, so we had to rely on our somewhat primitive topographical maps to guess where the portage trail was. More than once we had to back paddle when we realized we had missed such a trail. When we thought it was safe, we ran many rapids capsizing a couple times and breaking one of the paddles. We kept our supplies in tightly tied garbage bags anchored to the frame of the inside of the canoes so that if we capsized, they'd float. We made the whole 120-mile trip without injuries, but on one occasion after we had pushed the canoes upstream in shallow water, I noticed blood on the toe of my tennis shoe. Removing it, I discovered two leeches having a delicious meal between my toes.

That sporting trip included some fantastic northern light displays and close-up contact with nature. We spotted moose tracks near our tents upon rising one morning, Cranes, ducks, loons, eagles, hawks, and geese were plentiful, frequently swimming just ahead and beside us driving the beagle crazy. There were lots of beaver dams along the river. Two of the guys fished whenever we stopped, so we often had walleye for breakfast or dinner. Trying to determine what bait to use at the base of a dam, we cut open the first fish we caught and discovered what appeared to be a baby beaver or muskrat, not the kind of bait you'd find in a bait shop.

Soon after school finished in 1972, my wife and four-year-old son flew to Australia where I taught high school for a year. That brought me into contact with several new sports. In fact, I was the "coach" for Wednesday afternoon sports days for rugby and cricket. Being coach meant I only needed to show up to take roll and remain during the two hours of play to keep things under control. I realized what a knockdown, wild game rugby can be and that it isn't just the Australian version of American football. I'm not sure that I endured a complete cricket match which can include a tea break and last for more than one day, and it is not Australia's version of baseball. There was also lawn bowling on a bowling green. This sport was particularly popular among women's clubs. I attended the horse races in the small country town where I lived. Spectators simply stood around the track and heard and felt the rumbling of horses' feet as they approached and passed. On that occasion, I was only a few feet from the Australian prime minister.

I'm not one for spectator sports neither in a stadium nor on television. Maybe I watch a total of twenty minutes of college and professional football per year and half of that is at mandatory-attendance Super Bowl parties. With free tickets, I did attend two Detroit Lions games and three or four Detroit Pistons games. I'm slightly more involved with professional baseball having attended eight or ten Detroit Tigers games when my children were young and a half dozen more with foreign visitors. I once attended an exhibition professional tennis match in Detroit to watch John McEnroe. I don't recall who his opponent was. As for hockey, I have yet to watch one of those games. I once watched cliff divers in Acapulco. I guess that counts. As a child, we quite often went to the stock car races in Owosso, one of Pa's interests, and as long as we could get in free under the age of twelve, we continued to go. That same rule applied at the drive-in theater. Fortunately, or perhaps not, I was a runt and was able to pass as a twelve-year-old until I was fifteen. I got my lifetime fill of car races.

I mentioned earlier that no one had been injured on our canoe excursion in Canada, but real athletes generally expect injuries along the way. No pain, no gain? I have that "red badge of courage." One early summer evening playing very competitive one-on-one basketball in the driveway with our son, Mike, when he was a high school student, I slipped (or was I tripped?) and fell on the concrete. I knew instantly that I had broken my right wrist. I made it into the house and onto the couch without passing out. Martha had already gone to bed. Mike brought me an ice pack, but I told him I'd be all right, that it was just sprained. He went about other business. After a half hour or so, I felt relatively stable and decided to drive myself to a nearby clinic. An x-ray confirmed that my wrist was broken. They wrapped and splinted it and sent me home with directions to take a couple aspirins for pain. I slept well. The next morning, Martha and

I woke at about the same time. You can imagine her surprise waking to my huge wrapped wrist on the pillow next to her. That week I started summer classes. My classes had to listen well that semester because I couldn't write notes on the chalkboard.

Undoubtedly, the most spectacular spectator sporting event I attended was a professional soccer match in Strasbourg, France, the Strasbourg Blues vs the French town of Sedan. I know little about soccer rules, only that the ball has to somehow get into the net to score a goooooooal. That and the fact that there seem to be lots of serious injuries (or some award-winning acting?) Despite my naivete, I enjoyed every minute of this match. Here's why. The enthusiasm within the stadium was electric. As my French relative and I approached the stadium, we could hear tribal drums, horns, and loud chanting. Inside the stadium, the rowdy cheering continued non-stop throughout the match. Each team had its own cheer mob seated in a specifically designated area on opposite sides of the stadium. Most of this boisterous bunch of forty or fifty were men with a shirtless leader standing on a platform like a choir director leading rehearsed chants and cheers one after another. "Allez! Allez" Allez Blue!" They waved arms and flags and jumped and danced and tore off their shirts to wave as flags. Needless to say, my attention was more on this spectacle than on the match. I was distracted by the periodic "injury" of one of the players or the announcement of a goooooooooal! Don't ask me who won. I think it was a 2-2 tie.

Besides the several water sports I've already mentioned — a swim class at MSU, "hiking" through swamps in Georgia, waterskiing in Pentwater, and canoeing on the Turtle River — there are others. I'm not a fisherman, but I'm married to a fisherwoman who learned to fish at age of one on the Sioux River in South Dakota. There's a photo for proof. Thus, when we bought our cottage on a small lake near Gladwin, Michigan, I thought I'd give the relaxing sport of fishing a try. I was about as successful at that as I was at golf when I was in the army. Somehow Martha was hooking one bass or bluegill after another while the worm on my hook seemed to be out for a leisurely swim. Before long, our fishing excursions became Martha's serious catching of fish while I paddled the boat, anchored occasionally, and read poetry to her. Now THAT was relaxing! However, that's not the end of my fishing story. I have caught a few BIG ones on salmon fishing excursion boats in Lake Michigan — the real way to fish when someone else does all the work of baiting hooks, preparing the lines, getting us to where the fish are, and then interrupting my relaxation with a beer to announce that my line has a bite. Then for ten to fifteen minutes, I pretend I'm Hemingway hauling in a trophy. Voila! The excursion guide even cleans and fillets the salmon.

Two other water sports I've "mastered" are white-water rafting on the Youghiogheny River in the Allegany Mountains on the Pennsylvania/West Virginia border and parasailing in the South China Sea. The first was a camping/rafting trip on a Memorial Day weekend in 1985 with a small group of Martha's teaching colleagues. Our guide gave us some preliminary cautions should we happen to capsize, get stuck in rocks or on the river bank, or fall off the raft. There were four of us per raft, all with paddles and life preservers. We were to appoint one as the "captain" who would try to call out commands as we shot the rapids. My brother-in-law, Tom, thought he was our leader, but pictures of that excursion show me as the only one taking things seriously. The water was ice cold, still carrying snow melt from the mountains. I think there were four rafts in our group. We watched as others fell out of their rafts, got sprayed with ice water, and bailed water out of their rafts along the way. I think we got stuck once or twice in boulders, but we were the only ones to make the hour-and-a-half trip without losing anyone overboard. Parasailing in the South China Sea was at the invitation of one of my former Malaysian students whom I visited upon my return trip to Asia in 2009. It was as easy as catching salmon! Somebody else did all the work. I just sailed along with pleasure in the warm breeze over the very warm water. Delightful!

Bicycling is a sport, n'est pas? Though I haven't done the Tour de France, I have cycled many a kilometer in France — along the Seine in Paris and through the vineyards of Alsace. These were only relaxed, non-competitive, though quite lengthy, rides with French relatives. Under the planning and direction of a friend in Baltimore, with a group of four of us, I risked my life cycling across Maryland and New Jersey to the Atlantic, a great many of the miles along major highways with semi-trucks nearly sideswiping us. This same group biked for two days in the Appalachian Mountains, and due to poor planning, the first day was entirely uphill. Perhaps we were hiking and hauling our bikes more than we were riding them.

I guess if anything, running is my sport. It's certainly where my persistence and endurance seemed to surface in middle age. While I did much mandatory running in the army, I did none for years thereafter. Running or even jogging were not common exercises in the 70s. To see an adult running on the sidewalk or street would almost cause alarm. Was he running to escape or to help someone in danger? Then in the mid-1970s in my thirties, our miniature schnauzer slipped out of the yard and started racing toward a busy street a block away. I raced after him. When he decided to let me catch him halfway to the busy street, I found myself wheezing and gasping for air. Something told me that attention was needed.

I set out to do a little regular running at a park track near our home. At first, I ran, then walked, then ran, then walked for a mile. After several weeks, I was able to run a mile without resting. That accomplishment felt good, but my knees didn't! I was hardly able to climb steps to my second-floor office at school. Maybe running wasn't such a good idea. Maybe it's something people in their thirties shouldn't be taking up. I mentioned my complication to a couple men I knew to be runners. One asked if I stretched before and after running. I hadn't. He suggested several stretches, and for a couple weeks I did these stretches while my knees improved; then I started all over — walk, run, walk, run — for a mile with stretches before and after each outing. No pain!

And so for years, I ran two or three days a week, perhaps a total of six miles per week. Eventually, two-mile runs seemed quite short, so I went a little farther each time until in my fifties, I was running three or four miles several times a week — sixteen miles per week. Then quite coincidentally in 1997, I noticed an ad for a Lions Club charity race right in Birmingham two miles from home. I thought, "Since I'll be running anyway, why not try this?" So, I signed up for my first timed 10K race.

I was an innocent among real runners. I arrived in my ragged shorts and T-shirt an hour before the race began. I did stretches and studied a map of the running route as other runners began to arrive. The map identified "water" at three of four locations. What kind of race was this? I didn't want to run in wet shoes and socks. Of course, I soon realized that "water" meant that paper cups of water were offered to runners along the route. I also noticed that I seemed to be underdressed. Most runners had very colorful, "professional" matching shirt, shoes, shorts, and sweat band outfits. Never mind. I'd hide in the middle of the pack.

After the national anthem, the starting horn sounded, and we were on our way. Have you ever heard the sound of thousands of feet running on pavement? I hadn't. It was stimulating! After the first two miles, I realized that I had been running far faster than my usual pace and was already exhausted. I slowed down and plodded on as others passed me, but I never stopped. The route had some steep slopes. I chugged up them refusing to walk. By mile five, I was very aware that I had never run this far without walking partway. But on I went up one last steep slope toward the finish line, and I was "finished." I collapsed and sat on the sidewalk and leaned against a wall, sweating and catching my breath and watching the few last stragglers arrive. When I finally stood up, I found sore muscles all over my body and forgot about stretching. I was no longer a novice. I was initiated for what would become many more 5K and 10K races over time that have included dozens of Detroit Turkey Trots, lots of Detroit Marathon 5K runs and Detroit Riverfront 10K races. There have also been 10K's at the zoo and 5K's on Belle Isle and the fun Paczki Run in Hamtramck with a paczki and a beer at the end of the race. As I moved into my seventies, competition in my age category diminished, and I began to place in the top three finishers among ten or twelve runners. I began to think that sensible senior citizens are hanging up their running shoes, but have I ever been sensible? The truth is that I'm afraid to quit. I did quit for six months in 2010-11 after breaking three bones in my right foot from a non-running accident. Finally, I dared to run about sixty feet to the mailbox just to see if my foot would suddenly shatter. It didn't, and I was on my way again! In one 10K, I was both the first-place winner and the loser — the only one in my age category. In another, I was first among four runners defeating the third-place runner named Jesus Christ McNair. Imagine that I could run faster than Jesus! However, had we run on water, he would have had a distinct advantage.

Remember President George H. W. Bush skydiving at age ninety? What is it with old men and risk-taking ventures like this? I can only say that it's exhilarating. Though I've never skydived (yet), I did go hang-gliding in the Austrian Alps at age 69. Of course, I had a "coach" who did all the work. Once we were harnessed, he coached me to run as fast as I could toward the edge of a cliff drop-off and to look in the distance at a lake in the valley far below. I know it defies common sense to run off the edge of a cliff at full speed, but that's what launched us into a thrilling, pleasant ride, floating soundlessly for over an hour on air currents as an eagle would and landing just as gracefully in an open field in the valley. Then at age seventy-six, I found myself ziplining 300 feet above the rainforest floor in Costa Rica. What next?

At retirement in 2014, I located a fitness center not far from home to do maintenance upkeep and repair work in old age. There I do stretches, weights, and various machines especially those that physical therapists and doctors have suggested to ward off back and shoulder pain.

One last athletic endeavor that I've overlooked is hunting. I've been told that that qualifies as a sport. I did go squirrel and pheasant hunting on the farm as a teenager though I doubt that I ever shot the gun. However, I am earnest as a hunter of morel mushrooms but have eaten almost all of my trophies, so I have only photos for proof. Take my word for it.

Appendix

Shiawassee County was named for the river which runs through it, a Native American name which means "river that twists about".

Owosso, the largest city in Shiawassee County with a population of about 15,000, is named after Chief Wosso of the Ojibwe tribe. It was incorporated in 1859 — just 100 years before my high school graduation. Its two most famous native sons are Thomas E. Dewey, who ran twice for the US presidency against Franklin Roosevelt in 1944 and against Harry Tru-

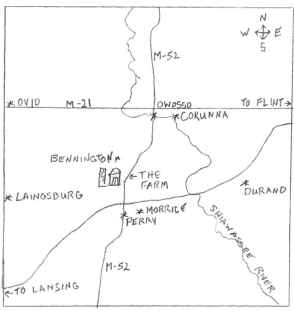

Shiawassee County Map

man in 1948, and James Oliver Curwood, a popular writer and silent movie producer in the early 20th century and later a conservationist in Michigan politics. Ma grew up in Owosso and graduated from Owosso High School in 1938. Our mailing address was Owosso where we did our banking, grocery shopping, and most other business.

Corunna is the county seat for Shiawassee County and location of McCurdy Park where the county fair was held each August in my childhood.

Perry has a population under 3,000, but for most of my young life, a sign at the village limits said, "Population 2001". This is where all my early education occurred since our farm was halfway between Owosso and Perry just a mile west of what today is M-52 and happened to be in the Perry school district.

Laingsburg is the village where we sold pickles to afford our one childhood bicycle, went swimming in nearby Round Lake, and played pinball machines as teens. Ma lived there when she passed away in 2001.

Ovid is the location of the farm where Pa worked as a hired man when he met Ma.

Life's Timeline to 1966

1938   Ma and Pa get married in Owosso —
        October 8th — and move to Benzonia
        Grand Ole Opry receives national recognition
        Nazi Germany annexes Austria and
        Czechoslovakia
        The ballpoint pen invented
        Teflon developed

1939   Dave born September 12th
Ma and Pa and Dave move to the 3888 West Brewer Road farm, which Grandpa Wilson helped them finance since Ma didn't go to college as did her brothers and sister
World War II starts in Europe
Batman comics introduced
Gone with the Wind as a movie

1940   Martha Christensen born February 27th
Franklin Roosevelt elected president for the third time
First McDonalds opens
Bugs Bunny introduced
Pennsylvania and Los Angeles freeways opened
First social security checks sent

1941   Ed born Saturday, November 15th
Pearl Harbor bombed December 7th

1942   Grandpa Ellis Wilson dies at age 55
Dick born November 8th
"White Christmas" released

1943   Antibiotics discovered
Pentagon Building completed

1944   Jude born July 5th
Ed held on Pa's shoulders to watch a Thomas Dewey presidential campaign whistle-stop in Owosso, Dewey's home town.
Grandpa Andrew Demerly dies April 18th
DNA discovered
D-Day June 6th

1945   Ed starts all-day kindergarten at
Perry Elementary

President Roosevelt dies April 12th

World War II ends with atomic bombs
on Japan

United Nations established

Fluoridated water introduced (Grand Rapids,
Michigan — first in the USA)

1946   Sal born January 5th

Uncle Lynn and Aunt Veda marry,
January 5th

Churchill coins words "Cold War" and
"Iron Curtain"

Benjamin Spock's first baby book

1947   Dead Sea Scrolls discovered

Jackie Robinson plays pro baseball on a
white team

Anne Frank's diary published

Sound barrier broken

Henry Ford dies

1948   President Truman reelected

Queen Elizabeth crowned as monarch

Gandhi assassinated

Modern state of Israel established

Orville Wright dies

Babe Ruth dies

1949   Communist government established
in China

45 rpm records introduced

William Faulkner wins the Nobel Prize
for literature

1950   Grandma Josephine Demerly dies April 9th
Korean War breaks out
"Peanuts" comic strip debuts

1951   We move into the new house
The term "rock 'n' roll" first used
Color TV marketed
The Catcher in the Rye published

1952   All five of us kids are baptized at the
Bennington Methodist Church on Dec 14
Eisenhower elected president
Queen Elizabeth II's coronation —
February sixth
The Old Man and the Sea published
Polio vaccine developed

1953   Korean War ends
TV Guide and Playboy introduced
Climbers reach the summit of Mt. Everest
for the first time

1954   Ed starts high school
Ed diagnosed with rheumatic fever
Ernest Hemingway receives the Nobel
for literature

1955   Rosa Parks refuses to move to the back
of the bus
Albert Einstein dies

1956   Elvis's career launched
First US hydrogen bomb test

1957   Dave's high school graduation
Mackinac Bridge opens
Sputnik launched

Little Rock school integration

Artificial heart and pacemaker introduced

Leave it to Beaver first airs

1958   Dave joins the army

Transatlantic passenger jet service launched

1959   Ed is salutatorian of his graduating class at
the new Perry High School

Ed starts classes at Michigan State and
moves into Bailey Hall

Year of the greatest DDT production
and use in the US

Alaska and Hawaii become states

Xerox copiers introduced

Castro takes control in Cuba —
February 16th

St. Laurence Seaway opens

Ford halts production of the Edsel

First Grammy Awards presented

1960   Ed lives and works at home for the
remaining years of college

Dick graduates from high school and
begins classes at MSU

Kennedy elected president

To Kill a Mockingbird published

1961   Ed chooses to continue in ROTC
to become an army officer

Ed joins the Pershing Rifles ROTC
Honorary Society

Berlin Wall built

Yuri Gagarin — first man to orbit the earth

MSU student Nancy Ann Fleming
wins Miss America

The IUD developed

Alan B Shepard first American in space

1962   Ed marches in Madison Square Garden
with MSU's ROTC precision drill team

Ed at summer boot camp at Fort Riley, Kansas

Cuban Missile Crisis in October

Vatican II convenes

Marilyn Monroe dies

First commercial satellite

John Steinbeck wins the Nobel for literature

US life expectancy reaches 70 for the first time

Eleanor Roosevelt and William Faulkner die

1963   Ed completes student teaching at Jackson
High School. Lives with Aunt Vivian's family

Ed's December graduation, bachelor's degree
in English/ French and History minors.
Certified to teach seventh to twelfth grades
in Michigan schools.

Commissioned as a 2nd lieutenant in the
Army Medical Service Corps

Civil Rights Act passes

MLK's Civil Rights March on Washington

Beatles launch their career

Supreme Court rules against prayer and
Bible recitation in public schools

President Kennedy is killed November 22

1964   Ed substitute teaches at Owosso, Laingsburg,
Perry, Morrice, Corunna, and Ovid

Ed reports for active duty at Fort Sam Houston, Texas, on March 8th

Ed is transferred to Fort Ord, California, in Monterey in June

Ed is assigned as the plans and operations officer at the Sixth Army post hospital

Dick and Janet marry June 27th

Ed completes airborne training at Fort Benning, Georgia

Johnson elected president

Confirmation that smoking causes cancer

1965   Ed completes ranger training

Sal and Dale marry July 24th

Combat troops sent to Vietnam

Sound of Music in theaters

Malcolm X assassinated

Winston Churchill dies

1966   Ed's honorable discharge from the army August 8th

Ed reports for Peace Corps training in Hilo, Hawaii, August 26th

Medicare begins

Birth control pills become available

Walt Disney dies

Author's Biographical Note

Ed Demerly retired after forty-six years of teaching — everything from fourth, fifth, and sixth grades, middle school, high school, and thirty-six years at Henry Ford College in Dearborn, Michigan, where he was the cofounder of the English Language Institute and the recipient of the Faculty Lectureship Award for his 1992 lecture on the parallels between Gangsta Rap and Walt Whitman's poetry. He taught for a year in Australia and for two years in Malaysia as a Peace Corps volunteer. Ed served in the army as an airborne ranger in the Medical Service Corps and is a past president of the National College English Association. He and his wife, Martha, live in Bloomfield Hills, Michigan, where in his retirement he is occupied with volunteer work that includes organizing public forums focused on justice and peace and counting frogs for the Rouge River Conservancy. As a runner, and now nearly 80, he finds it's much easier than in the past to place first in his age group in 5K and 10K races. He's a gardener of okra, cherries, asparagus, rhubarb, raspberries, peas, apples, flowers, and so much more — still a farm boy.

Made in the USA
Monee, IL
30 March 2023